D0817874

PREVENTING HOME ACCIDENTS

"*Preventing Home Accidents* is a simple-to-read, easy-to-follow guide to reducing the leading causes of injuries—those that occur outside the workplace. Developing and implementing a basic home safety plan will provide a manyfold return on reducing pain and suffering for the readers and their families."

— Leo F. Hamilton
Global Director: Safety, Health, Environment
DuPont Company

Ordering

Trade bookstores in the U.S. and Canada please contact:

Publishers Group West
1700 Fourth Street, Berkeley CA 94710
Phone: (800) 788-3123   Fax: (800) 351-5073

Hunter House books are available at bulk discounts for
textbook course adoptions; to community, health-care, and government
organizations; and for special promotions and fund-raising.
For details please contact:

Special Sales Department
Hunter House Inc., PO Box 2914, Alameda CA 94501-0914
Phone: (510) 865-5282, ext. 301   Fax: (510) 865-4295
E-mail: ordering@hunterhouse.com

Individuals can order our books from most bookstores,
by calling **(800) 266-5592**, or from our website at
www.hunterhouse.com

PREVENTING HOME ACCIDENTS

DAN HANNAN, CSP

With a Foreword by
BOB VILA

PUBLISHERS

A Quick & Easy Guide

Hunter House Inc., Publishers
PO Box 2914
Alameda CA 94501-0914

Library of Congress Cataloging-in-Publication Data
Hannan, Dan.
Preventing home accidents : a quick and easy safety reference / Dan Hannan.—1st ed.
p. cm.
ISBN 978-0-89793-607-1 (pbk.)
1. Home accidents—Prevention. I. Title.
TX150.H36 2011
363.13—dc23   2011037489

Project Credits

Cover Design: Jinni Fontana	Publicity and Marketing: Sean Harvey
Book Production: John McKercher	Rights Coordinator: Candace Groskreutz
Copy Editor: Heather Wilcox	Customer Service Manager: Christina Sverdrup
Proofreader: John David Marion	Order Fulfillment: Washul Lakdhon
Managing Editor: Alexandra Mummery	Administrator: Theresa Nelson
Acquisitions Assistant: Elizabeth Kracht	Computer Support: Peter Eichelberger
Senior Marketing Associate: Reina Santana	Publisher: Kiran S. Rana

Printed and bound by Bang Printing, Brainerd, Minnesota
Manufactured in the United States of America

9 8 7 6 5 4 3 2 1   First Edition   11 12 13 14 15

Contents

For immediate access, Resource sections are included at the end of each chapter, not at the end of the book. You can download a consolidated list from the Hunter House website: Visit hunterhouse.com, search for *Preventing Home Accidents*, and go to the "Download Resources" link.

Foreword

by Bob Vila

Whenever I'm asked what's the most important consideration when tackling a do-it-yourself or home improvement project, my first response is safety. Throughout my years as TV host of *This Old House, Bob Vila Home Again,* and *Bob Vila,* I worked with enough construction workers, plumbers, electricians, carpenters, and contractors to know that even the most seasoned professional needs to remain mindful of safety when it comes to handling tools and managing job site procedures. That goes for homeowners too, who, when tackling even the simplest of DIY projects and home maintenance updates and repairs, can be setting themselves up for mild or serious injuries—or worse.

While most home safety is little more than good common sense, there is a tendency to overlook the obvious. How many times have you stepped down from a ladder and miscalculated the last step? Or what about climbing too high on a ladder and losing your balance? Have you ever attempted to replace an electrical outlet, install a dimmer switch, or hang a chandelier only to discover that the power you thought you turned off was still "live"? You would not be alone.

And, let's not overlook the home workshop. A lot of people assume they know how to use power tools but never bother to read the instruction manual or manufacturer's safety warnings. I can't tell you how many stories I've heard about a table saw kicking back a piece of wood and causing serious injury to the operator. Even drills can cause wrist damage over time if not handled properly. When it comes to preventing eye injuries, which can often be catastrophic, the solution is as simple as putting on a pair of protective goggles. Yet how often is that simple safety requirement ignored? There are so many comfortable, inexpensive goggles on the market today—including bifocal and lighted varieties—that there is no excuse not to safeguard your vision every chance possible.

In *Preventing Home Accidents* you will find a wealth of valuable, detailed information on everything from best safety practices for using power and hand tools to the proper way to store, use, and dispose of aerosol spray cans, unused paints, and household cleaning supplies. You will gain a better understanding—and appreciation—of electricity and why tackling any project that involves "flipping a switch" on a circuit breaker may be best left to the professionals. There are tips and advice on improving your home's indoor air quality by eliminating harmful toxins and hazards like lead and mold, and safeguards you should know about yard projects…like determining where underground power lines and pipes are located before planting a tree or sinking a deck post.

The book is an interactive and informational guide for learning how to identify and correct hazards in the home, complete with reviewing checklists, instructional exercises, valuable website resources, and useful toll-free hotline numbers. Learn what every home first-aid kit should include, the importance of maintaining smoke and carbon monoxide detectors, and why every family should have a disaster preparedness plan in case of emergency.

One of the most important things to remember when tackling any home project is to take your time. Think about what you're doing and examine every step of the project so that you can analyze what is involved and, more importantly, what may go wrong. And be sure to keep this book as part of your home's reference library. I know I plan to.

Bob Vila
BobVila.com

Preface

While it is generally true that "every man's home is his castle," living in your home may not be nearly as safe as you think it is. The numbers are staggering—annually 46 percent of all accidental deaths occur in the home, outpacing automobile and workplace fatalities combined.[1] Nearly 55,000 homeowners fall victim to a fatal injury in the home every year, and 13 million others suffer disabling injuries from falls, fires, electric shock, poisoning, and other means. These figures, along with the fact that individuals' behavior is responsible for more than 80 percent of all accidents, led me to write this book. Nearly everyone has experienced an accident or injury in the home that resulted in stitches, a broken finger, or even a broken leg. In hindsight, was the cause of that injury the stupid chair or the choice you made to stand on it instead of a ladder to change the light bulb? Conclusion: *You* are responsible for your accidents and injuries, and *you* allow your home to be far more dangerous than it has to be.

[1] National Safety Council, "Injury Facts," 2010.

You probably don't pay much attention to the safety condition of your home, much as you don't believe you will get into a car accident on any given day—it just happens sometimes. Unlike the road, your home is a more controllable environment. You can be proactive and significantly improve the safety condition of your home by learning how to recognize and eliminate hazards. You will come to understand that your behavior is at the root of your "state of safety." This book educates and then empowers you to think about and perform safety measures to maintain a safe and healthful home. I don't point out the obvious, such as not sticking your finger in an outlet. Rather, I want to build your safety knowledge and decision-making ability on the old adage, "Teach a man to fish and you feed him for a lifetime." I've kept the chapters short, to the point, and filled with information you can apply in your own life. My goal is to improve your safety awareness and inspire you to think and behave more safely in all that you do.

A Personal Message

It is difficult to show that you personally care for others through just the text in a book, although "caring" is pretty important in safety matters. Those safety professionals who are great at what they do succeed by changing behavior and "selling" safety by showing they care. They show they care by talking to the worker, not at them; by taking an accident and turning it into a teaching moment; and by being there day in and day out to help look after the well-being of the workforce, so they all can go home to their families at the end of each day. Genuinely caring for others creates an environment of respect and pride. Do I personally care about you? In this case, I don't need to know you personally for both of us to win. My measure of success comes from knowing that someone somewhere will get enough out of this book to prevent a loved one from experiencing a disabling injury or dying in the home. For this reason, though, I do

The Hannan castle (Illustration by John Grancorvitz)

want to know that I made a difference. I need to hear from you about how you applied the information in this book and whether it helped improve the quality of your life. Please go to my website at www.danshomesafety.com and give me your comments. Let me know if I can share your success story (with or without your name) on my website for others to see and be inspired by. I do care about helping people not injure themselves or others. Although I can't get to know you well enough to call you a friend, I believe we still have a bond as we share the same mission—using safety to protect the ones we care about.

Sincerely,

Dan

Important Note

The safety information provided in this book contains suggestions and recommendations based on professional experience, interpretation of occupational safety regulations, and industry best practices. Every home presents unique safety conditions and hazards. This book cannot account for all hazards, conditions, and circumstances. It is possible that you will misunderstand, misinterpret, or not apply this information properly. For this reason, the author, as well as the publisher, editors, and professionals who are quoted (or referred to) in this book, assume no liability for injuries or damages that result from the use of the information in this book.

You are encouraged to seek qualified professional help when you have questions or lack the technical background or skill to implement the suggested safety practices in this book. If you have any questions concerning the application of the information described in this book, consult a qualified safety professional. Note that safety professionals may have differing opinions, also that advances in safety and technology are made very quickly, so some of the information presented may also become outdated.

Acknowledgments

The author would like to acknowledge the following individuals for their contribution to this book: Duane, my brother the English teacher, a big thanks for your editing help. Scott H., my safety colleague, thanks for your technical review. I value your opinion greatly. Cynthia Roth, ETC, for help with describing safe lifting and body mechanics.

Contributions

Thank you to all of the following manufacturers and organizations that contributed to the images in the book.

Introduction

Do you believe that accidents "just happen," or do you believe that they are a series of preventable events? Nearly anything can be made to be 100 percent safe, but sometimes doing so requires costly safety measures and personal commitment to the goal. In the workplace, therein lies the challenge—putting in place safety controls to significantly reduce injuries without breaking the bank or impeding productivity. An ethical battle between the safety professional and the company owner may develop

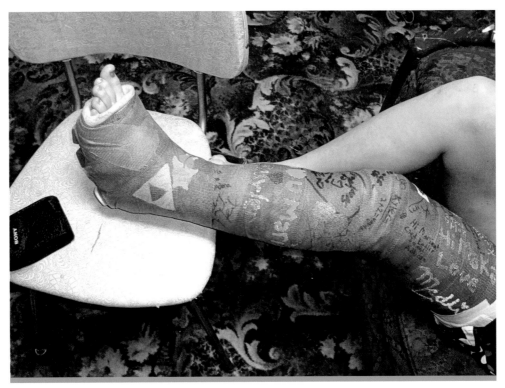

The downside of home injuries—having to cancel the family vacation!

regarding the price tag for safety. An individual's home is no different. As you read this book and wish to improve your home's safety conditions, you will be faced with the same decision of how much safety is enough, based on cost and effort. Be assured that any attention and money you apply is better than doing nothing.

At least 80 percent of accidents result from unsafe behaviors, such as ignoring a broken piece of equipment, disabling a safety feature, not wearing safety glasses, or not reading the owner's manual before using a power tool. To illustrate risky behavior, safety trainers commonly ask leading questions, such as, "How many of you use your safety training and equipment when working at heights on the job"? Every hand goes up as it should. Yet when those same workers who also hunt are asked, "How many of you climb into your deer stand every year during hunting season without being tied-off to the tree?" again, nearly every hand goes up. These workers choose to ignore their safety knowledge when dealing with a familiar job-related type of hazard in their personal lives. Why?

This book is not a listing of safety tips and tricks. It is intended to educate homeowners on why and where home hazards exist and then to

provide the tools to eliminate them. The book adapts a number of proven occupational safety principles and techniques for home use. You will be challenged to get to know your home better and develop a proactive rather than reactive stance to staying safe. You will also be challenged to think about the choices you make and your behavior. It won't hurt a bit. Chapters are organized into four sections:

1. **Education:** providing you with an understanding of where dangers lurk in the home and how to identify them
2. **Recommended Practices:** proven home safety practices to correct identified hazards
3. **Proactive Safety:** a safety checklist to take ownership of your home's safety condition (this section does not appear in all chapters)
4. **Resources:** a listing of useful organizations, associations, and manufacturers that can provide additional safety information

For those of you who work in a safety-conscious workplace, your employers should be tickled to know that you are taking safety seriously at home. The employer "off-the-job" safety movement has gained momentum over the last ten years. The movement challenges the employees to take their safety knowledge—and, in some cases, safety equipment—home with them at the end of the day. After all, there is a real cost to the employer whose employee cannot show up for work on Monday because they had an accident with a chain saw over the weekend. Companies that possess world-class safety programs preach and expect "personal ownership" of safety practice—safety is a shared responsibility. This mind-set should not stop once the worker gets home.

Finally, safety is not about thinking of yourself as being a "safety nerd" who religiously wears their safety glasses, steel-toe boots, and earplugs when they mow the grass. The reward for placing safety first is that you will still have all your fingers, toes, and eyes at the end of the day. Don't be intimidated or embarrassed by choosing to live safely. Take pride in applying safety principles in everything you do. The benefits will be returned many times over.

Safety—A Family Affair

Safety professionals who complete inspections on construction work sites are resigned to the fact that their observations reflect just specific points in time. Even if a safety hazard is not spotted right now, it is likely that one will appear tomorrow or even in the next hour. That is the challenge with construction—the hazards are always changing.

Safety for Life

A home, too, is a dynamic place. Seasons change, people come and go, and by "living" in your home, you unknowingly introduce hazards or bring to life ones that have been dormant. Furthermore, the sense of familiarity and comfort you have in your home often leads to safety complacency.

By actively practicing the safety methods described in this book, you will develop and improve your ability to recognize and correct hazards. You will be proud when you do discover a hazard, even a small one, and take action to correct it. However, you can't be everywhere all the time. That is why safety is a family thing. If you enlist everyone's help, everyone will benefit.

Progressive companies with world-class safety programs understand the benefits of instilling responsible safety behavior at work that then carries into the home. The key to developing good habits and behaviors at home is to create an environment where safety is practiced and expected.

It is never too late to start learning about safety, but learning about it earlier is better. Would you rather teach your children the virtues of saving and spending wisely when they are five years old or fifteen years old? The following story illustrates why earlier is better: One day after I picked up my six-year-old daughter from school, we crossed a set of nearby railroad tracks. She scolded me and said, "Daddy, you didn't stop, look, and listen." I asked her to repeat what she had said and then asked where she had learned that saying. She said that a person from the railroad company had given a presentation at her school. What do I do now every time I cross railroad tracks in rural areas? I stop, look, and listen. This reinforces good safety behavior in me, which trickles down to her and to everyone else in my car. Likewise, the way to best teach a young person how to drive is to lead by example. From the first day you put your children into their car seats, they are watching you. As they grow,

The author presenting a home-safety message to his daughter's kindergarten class

they will likely develop habits that reflect yours: "If it's OK for Mom or Dad to do it, then it's OK for me." Getting all family members involved in thinking about and applying safety in the home will help you develop a collective culture of safety and pass on skills that will last a lifetime.

Success Is up to You!

For safety to succeed in a large company, everyone from upper management to part-time employees must buy into the concept and implement it. Your commitment at home will certainly make you safer, but to really hit the safety effort out of the park, everyone needs to believe it is a good idea. You need to champion the effort and be a leader. Step up to this challenge and the rewards will be realized for a lifetime.

(Photo courtesy of the Family Worship Center)

How do you get involvement from your kids, significant other, relatives, or neighbors?

1. **Create the Atmosphere** An atmosphere of safety is created by leading by example and showing a commitment. To make the atmosphere stick, deliver safety information in a fun, interesting, and relevant way. Work toward goals and offer rewards when they are attained (see the "Recommended Practices" section below). Encourage ideas and participation from all members of your household.

2. **Observe and Correct** The active part of practicing safety involves the identification and removal of hazards using hazard-analysis techniques (explained in the next chapter). A good safety profes-

sional finds value in evaluating a hazard condition through the eyes of the person exposed to it/the user. For example, observing how a user interacts with electricity may bring to light how an accident could occur and how to best prevent that from happening. When fixing a hazardous condition, again involve the user. To achieve the greatest level of safety cooperation, work with the user to come up with a solution to overcome the hazard.

3. **Implement and Communicate** Identify an unsafe condition, correct it, and then communicate with all those who are or may be affected by the change. For instance, if you have just installed a new safety feature in the garage to

prevent items stored on shelving from falling down, let everyone know how it works and that it must be used every time to be successful. Get everyone in your family to buy into a "safety-first" com-

mitment by challenging everyone to watch out for each other.

4. **Evaluate** Perform checkups at regular intervals to decide whether the safety fix is working correctly. This feedback loop is important to ensure continued success.

Recommended Practices

☑ Pick a safety topic for the week or month to focus on and discuss it at dinner time. This could include topics found in this book. Especially good are those "what-if" situations, such as a fire or severe weather event. Remember that people have to see, hear, or do something seven times on average before it is committed to memory.

☑ Challenge family members to find news articles related to home hazards. A good example might be a report on a home fire caused by poorly maintained smoke alarms. The topic may be seasonal. For example, during the winter of 2010–11 it snowed particularly heavily in the upper Midwest, and this caused homeowners to have to remove snow from their roofs to prevent excessive snow and ice buildup. What ensued were weekly news reports of people falling off their roofs, and in at least one instance, a homeowner fell to his death.

☑ Games are a fun way to learn. Create crossword or seek-and-find puzzles related to safety, and have a contest to see who can complete the puzzle most quickly. See the Resources section below for places to find free safety games.

☑ Every month have the entire family work together to complete a home "hazard hunt" during which you search for hazards based on the checklists found in this book. Work in teams and offer "fabulous, wonderful prizes," such as a trip for ice cream, if five or more hazards are found.

☑ Finally, champion off-the-job safety by encouraging your employer to challenge its workforce to bring safety home. Start by getting the

A safety calendar created from drawings by the children of workers helps them bring the idea of safety to their homes. (Calendar courtesy of Hunt Electric Corporation)

workers and their families involved. Have the children create a company safety calendar from pictures that they draw. Each month can represent a different safety theme—preventing fires, wearing a bicycle helmet, and so forth. Safety is a way to demonstrate care and compassion for your fellow workers.

RESOURCES

An outstanding video by VitalSmarts demonstrates how to get children to listen to directions and improve their cooperative behavior. The video can be found at http://www.crucialskills.com/2009/09/all-washed-up.

The National Safety Council offers a monthly magazine publication (through employer participation) specifically promoting safety off the job. A subscription mailed to the home allows everyone in the home to benefit. For more information go to http://www.nsc.org /news_resources/nsc_publications /Pages/NSC_publications.aspx.

 To make customized, *free* crossword, seek-and-find, and other puzzles, go to http://www.puzzle maker.com.

 For younger kids, the Consumer Product Safety Commission (CPSC) offers games, printable coloring pages, and more resources regarding home safety at http://www.cpsc.gov/kids/kidsafety /index.html.

Safety arts and crafts for younger kids can be found at http://www.dltk-kids.com/safety/index .htm.

The Centers for Disease Control and Prevention (CDC) provides fact sheets and recommendations about a variety of home-safety topics at http://www.cdc.gov/homeand recreationalsafety/index.html.

The National Institute for Occupational Safety and Health (NIOSH) promotes off-the-job safety through employer programs. More information can be found at http:// www.cdc.gov/niosh/TWH.

Children's Hospitals and Clinics of Minnesota provides information on a variety of child safety topics at http://www.childrensmn.org /Services/Emergency/MakingSafe Simple.

I post current home-safety articles and information on my website at http://www.danshome safety.com.

CHAPTER 2

Know Your Castle

Your home provides you with shelter, entertainment, and many fond memories. You probably spend half your waking hours and nearly all your sleeping hours in your home. You should know your home better than anyone else does. Your state of home safety is determined by how your home is constructed and functions and how you live within it. Taking some time to understand how your home operates will add greatly to your safety bottom line.

Home Construction

Like a car, a home is constructed according to certain design standards for life-safety protection. These standards, or codes, are partly based on such elements as the home's architectural design, fire-safety requirements, and geographic location. For cars, such safety features as side airbags, backup cameras, and antilock brakes are available but come with sometimes-hefty price tags. If you purchased your home after it was built, you have little say regarding the safety features that went into its construction. Being able to overcome safety threats through engineering design is always preferred but not always financially feasible. For instance, not many homeowners have the funds to install a fire-sprinkler system—a huge plumbing and remodeling project. The one thing that a homeowner can control 100 percent of the time is their behavior and personal approach to safety. You must therefore be aware of your home's safety shortcomings and, at the very least, learn to live safety smart. For instance, an increased electrical demand from a new entertainment center in the basement may put a strain on your home's entire electrical system, adding to the risk of an electrical fire. Understanding the construction of your home and its limitations will better help you avert a safety mishap.

A home built of bricks may be structurally stronger than one built of straw, but it may be no safer. Your home functions as the sum of its parts. These parts are designed and manufactured independently but are assembled to perform safely together. Glass, metal, wood, plastic, and many other types of materials have gone into your home's construction. How structurally safe your home is depends largely on the building code at the time of construction which is largely determined by where and when the structure was built. Since the building code dictates the use of certain building materials and construction processes designed to make the structure safe, generally speaking, the newer the home, the safer its construction due to code improvements. Building code is put into law at the city, state, or national level. Code is then enforced locally by building officials throughout the home's construction/renovation. Commercial dwellings, but not private homes, are inspected on a regular basis to ensure safety-code compliance. Contractors are required to obtain permits for construction projects, which prompt

A home is constructed of many different materials that function safely together.

building officials to inspect the structures. The owners of homes that are not built or remodeled according to code risk being fined or having their homes declared unsafe/unfit to live in.

Homeowners who perform certain work themselves ("do-it-yourselfers, or DIYers") and who do not obtain permits or complete the work according to code risk serious consequences. Bypassing safety requirements within

Homeowners who perform their own remodeling work are challenged to understand their home's construction and perform the work according to building code.

the building code doubles the homeowners' hazard stakes: Not only may the houses be at greater risk for damage, but insurance companies may not honor future claims if they determine that the homes were not remodeled or repaired according to code.

Even professional contractors may cut safety corners to save money and avoid using the most compliant methods or materials when working on your home. Remember, safety products and processes come at a cost, and safety is often the first thing to go when profit margins are tight. When you are evaluating a contractor to work on your home, read the fine print of their service contract and consider the following details:

- Hire a contractor who is licensed and bonded to ensure that they adhere to professional standards and have the financial guarantee to back their work.

- Investigate the contractor to look for any prior issues regarding their work. Contact the Better Business Bureau or local home builders associations to determine whether any complaints have been registered. Ask for several customer references from the contractor for recently completed projects. Talk to those references about their experiences with the contractor.

- Look for language in the service contract that specifically states that the construction will be completed according to current building code, design standards, and safety regulations.

Knowing Where Things Are

The middle of the night is the wrong time to ask yourself, "How do I shut off the water to the dishwasher that's leaking?" If you are in the process of building your home or are the first owner of a newly constructed home, get a set of blueprints from the contractor who built it. Spend some time with the contractor to identify where the electrical circuits are run within the walls and ceiling, the location of ventilation ducts, and where the natural gas lines and water and sewer lines are laid out. If necessary, draw on the

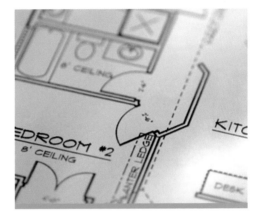

Blueprints are a good way to keep track of elements of your home's mechanical systems, such as water and gas lines, electrical circuits, and drain lines. (Image courtesy of Villa Custom Homes)

This photo of a basement ceiling shows hot and cold water lines, sewer and vent drains, and telephone and electrical wire. Can you tell which is which?

Mark water lines, gas lines, and electrical circuits for ease of identification.

Intake and exhaust pipes can be located on the roof or the side of the home. Know the function of each pipe and keep them free of debris.

blueprint in different colors to identify the different utilities. Guessing about the location of an electrical line behind a wall when you're driving a nail to hang a picture is not safety smart. Don't forget about the buried utilities outside! These can be located with the assistance of your local utility providers—electrical, natural gas, water, and so forth. Look on your utility bills for phone numbers or website addresses and contact the companies to help locate your lines.

Mark and label valves and switches with pieces of masking tape and a permanent marker. For example, at the control valve, label hot and cold water pipes and describe what they control (for example, "cold water, upstairs toilet"). If you have drop ceilings, remove some ceiling panels and look in the space above them to establish the layout of the utilities. Don't forget about the outside of your home. Locate any ventilation and exhaust pipes. Your house breathes by taking in fresh outside air and discharging combustion gases from the furnace, water heater, or clothes dryer if they are powered by natural gas or propane. Intake and exhaust pipes are typically located on the roof or the side of the home. Familiarizing yourself with your home's structure requires effort, but you only have to do it once.

Insurance

Accident preparedness can take many forms including the use of insurance to manage the risks associated with the loss of property and life. When you've done what you can to prevent an accident from happening, insurance provides additional piece of mind for those things that cannot be controlled or anticipated.

Almost all of us own some type of insurance—home, auto, health, or life. For a homeowner, properly insuring your home is a means of protecting your largest physical asset. In order for insurance to be effective and do its job, the type and amount of insurance you obtain needs to be considered carefully. As with all insurance policies you want to make sure you understand completely what type of accidents or losses are covered. If you are not sure about any of the terms or conditions of your policy, sit down with your agent and have them explain it to you in detail. It is too late and after the fact if your home is underwater from a flood and the "water damage" coverage in your policy only covers a broken water pipe.

You pay a premium to own insurance that may be deducted (escrowed) from your monthly mortgage payment. Your premium is primarily established based on the value of the home, its geographic location, and the amount of coverage (monetary limits of liability) that you choose. In order for your insurance to be the best risk-management tool that it can be, carefully consider the following four principal aspects of insurance:

1. **Type of loss covered:** details what the insurance is actually protecting, such as the structure (home), belongings (personal property), and medical bills if someone gets hurt on your property.

Courtesy of Hollins, Raybin and Weissman—Attorneys at Law

2. **Deductible:** the amount of money that comes out of your pocket before your coverage kicks in. A higher deductible usually means a lower cost of insurance.
3. **Amount of coverage and limits:** the specified dollar amount to be paid out by the insurance company for the loss per occurence (event).
4. **Exclusions or limitations:** specific restrictions by which the coverage may be limited or denied. Understand these thoroughly!

One final thought regarding home insurance: You should give serious consideration to purchasing an umbrella policy. This type of policy provides coverage when the limits of liability (maximum monetary payout) falls short on your primary policy. All-hazard umbrella policies can be purchased to cover both your home and autos, and they can provide one million dollars or more of coverage. The cost of such coverage is often very reasonable. It doesn't take a large accident these days to result in a claim that may exceed your standard policy limits and break your bank.

Recommended Practices

☑ If you don't know where your utility services are located or how they work, contact a home contractor in your area to help educate you. Understand valves, switches, pumps, and other critical mechanical systems. Mark and label them accordingly to aid in understanding what controls what. This knowledge will go a long way in preventing an accident.

☑ Codes are developed for safety and are updated regularly. If you do not understand the building code or cannot perform a home project according to code, hire a professional contractor to complete the work.

☑ Develop a general sense of where outside utilities enter your home. Periodically check visible utilities, such as overhead power lines or vent pipes, for fallen branches or signs of damage. Vent pipes can become blocked by snow, animal nests, or a child's abandoned toy or rag. Keep intake and exhaust pipes clear of debris.

RESOURCES

 The National Association of Home Builders provides a link to state building associations that can offer information and recommendations for contractor services at http://www.nahb.org/local_association _search_form.aspx.

 The Better Business Bureau provides information regarding contractor complaints at http:// www.bbb.org/us/find-a-bbb.

 The Home Safety Council is a national nonprofit organization that advocates home safety and provides additional information regarding home construction safety at http://www.homesafetycouncil.org /AboutUs/au_aboutus_w001.asp.

 Bob Vila offers educational do-it-yourself guidance at http://www.bobvila.com.

 The Insurance Information Institute provides the general public with valuable information for better understanding types of insurance and how to read an insurance policy at http://www.iii.org/about.

 I post current home-safety articles and information on my website at http://www.danshome safety.com.

Safety Basics

Attention! Your safety-basics training starts **now!**

Simply put, being "safe" is a condition of being free from harm or danger. Can you ever get your home into a state of being truly "safe"? Certainly, your goal should be to strive for a home environment that is completely free of hazards. That may be a tall order, but don't get discouraged. The first step to achieving your goal is to improve your ability to recognize hazards and address unsafe behavior.

An old adage says, "An ounce of prevention is worth a pound of cure." Why is it necessary to be proactive about preventing accidents at home? Home-related incidents account for the single largest category of unintentional deaths (see Figure 3.1). Deaths result from falls, electrocutions, hand and power tool accidents, chemical exposures, fires, and other preventable situations. Your attitude toward safety and your ability to spot a hazard and prevent an injury in the home will go a long way toward keeping you or a family member from joining these ranks.

You might ask yourself, "Why should I fix something that isn't broken?" Stated another way, "I've never had an accident at home, so why should I waste time trying to prevent one?" Think of proactive safety like taking a defensive driving course. It may not completely eliminate the chances of you getting into an accident, but it sure helps to minimize the chances!

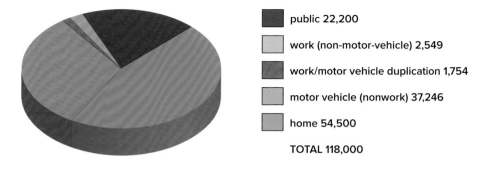

- public 22,200
- work (non-motor-vehicle) 2,549
- work/motor vehicle duplication 1,754
- motor vehicle (nonwork) 37,246
- home 54,500

TOTAL 118,000

FIGURE 3.1 Percentage of deaths by location (©National Safety Council® "Injury Facts®," 2010 Edition)

Your Behavior — What's Your Risk Tolerance?

The decisions you make, expressed through your behavior, are responsible for many outcomes in your life, good and bad. For example, the decision to save or to not save for retirement determines your standard of living, now and in the future; to wear or to not wear your seat belt while driving impacts the severity of injuries suffered in a car accident; to overreach while standing on an extension ladder instead of moving it to the desired location results in a disabling home injury. A number of factors influence the way you make decisions, and when it comes to safety, risk is a primary driver. Everyone equates risk differently, which is why some enjoy skydiving while others do not.

Over time, the results of your decisions forms your behaviors and habits. For instance, look at the photo showing a crowd running from a bull on the loose in the streets in Pamplona, Spain. Safety professionals, and most everyone else, would consider this a risky behavior. The question: "Will these citizens do this again next year"? The answer: "Yes," *if* they

If there is no negative result, risky behavior is often repeated. (Photo courtesy of IBTimes)

succeed without an injury. Without an undesirable consequence, they will repeat the behavior again and again. You are no different. Bad habits are hard to break, especially when you don't properly perceive risk or have been lucky enough to avoid getting hurt up to this point. What makes home safety particularly challenging is that the home is a relaxed environment, which lends itself to safety complacency—definitely a dangerous behavior. As you read this book, take a look inward and honestly ask yourself or your significant other, "Am I a risk taker, and can I behave more safely?"

Your Behavior—Safety Is Hard to Get Excited About

Compared to at-risk behavior, safe behavior is often uncomfortable, inconvenient, and less fun. Being safe doesn't require a suit of armor! (Photo courtesy of Wikimedia Commons)

The goal of many safety professionals in educating the workforce is to instill a "*want*-to-be-safe" rather than a "*have*-to-be-safe" attitude. By slowly changing your perception of safety and thus your behavior, you will find comfort in knowing that you won't be the one at risk of losing an eye, toe, or finger before the job is done. In the end, the challenge for the homeowner and even the paid worker is to overcome the mental side of staying safe—being motivated to think about and to perform safety measures from start to finish on every task. Traditional thinking says doing things safely is not fun, costs time and money, and is cumbersome. Be prepared to be challenged and open to changing your way of thinking about safety. Once you have armed yourself with new safety knowledge, it is time to get just a little bit excited.

Your Behavior—Wow, That Was Close!

Nearly 80 percent of all accidents result from behavior (actions), while 20 percent result from unsafe conditions (such as a defective electrical cord). In the safety-professional world, close calls are referred to as "near hits," such as when a dump truck almost backs over someone. Near hits are valuable in determining unsafe trends. If a trend does exist, corrections to the system can be made, such as offering more safety training, designing a different procedure, or purchasing new equipment.

Nearly 2 million unsafe acts are the precursors to deaths (see Figure 3.2). You will likely never commit 2 million unsafe acts in your lifetime, but collectively homeowners across the country easily surpass this number in any given year. Will you be the one to commit the 2-millionth unsafe act resulting in a fatality? The triangle below depicts the estimated number of occurrences of each type of accident that yields a fatality.

FIGURE 3.2 Incident-occurrence frequencies

Your Behavior—The ABCs

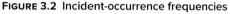

Do you ever wonder why some people are accident prone? They may be accident prone due the way they think and act (or fail to act). In this book the "ABCs" refer to the mental and physical steps that occur en route to an accident outcome:

1. **Activator:** the event(s) that triggers the mind to think in an unsafe way
2. **Behavior:** the action(s) resulting from the activator trigger
3. **Consequence:** the outcome or result of the behavior (injury!)

An example might be: Joe wakes up in the morning ready to begin his project of building a small cabinet for his basement entertainment system. During breakfast, he gets into a heated argument with a family member (**Activator**). Joe goes into the garage and unpacks the circular saw power tool to cut plywood. He is still fuming from the argument and rehashes the conversation in his head. He does not take the time to properly set the cutting depth on the saw blade and does not use sawhorses but instead cuts the sheet of plywood on blocks on the ground (**Behavior**). Joe kneels to make the cut, and the saw kicks back when it hits one of the blocks on the ground, cutting a deep gash in his leg (**Consequence**).

Had Joe used sawhorses and set the saw to cut at the proper depth, the injury would not have happened. The root cause of the accident was not the improper set-up for cutting the plywood but rather Joe's unsafe mindset. It takes a tremendous amount of awareness and discipline to step back and self-check your safety frame of mind prior to a task. These skills can be learned and improved.

An **Activator** can be anything that causes you to lose focus on the task and safety, such as stress or using a cell phone.

TABLE 3.1. Activators

ACTIVATOR EXAMPLES	BEHAVIOR EXAMPLES	CONSEQUENCE
frustration (stupid knife!) ⟶	rushing ⟶	injury
fatigue (lack of sleep) ⟶	loss of focus ⟶	injury
complacency (same old thing) ⟶	loss of focus ⟶	injury

Types of Hazards

Accidents result from hazards. It is helpful to know what type of hazard is present to avoid an accident. Hazards can be grouped together based on their common types. Preventative measures are very similar for grouped hazard types. For instance, where rotating parts are the hazard (for example, a grinding wheel or a table saw blade), a key component of safety is making sure the guard surrounding the rotating part is working properly and is positioned correctly.

The following examples illustrate the four most common hazard types that lead to accidents:

1. **mechanical:** rotating parts, coiled springs, or the swing of a hammer
2. **chemical:** gases, liquids, solids (such as propane, mineral spirits, dry pesticide, or fertilizer)
3. **physical:** heat, cold, electricity, noise,
4. **biological:** bug bites, poison ivy, sewage, blood

Remember these four main hazard categories as you apply the technique of finding hazards.

Finding Hazards

Uncovering a hazard can be accomplished by routine inspection or, in the case of a new project, at the start with a little planning. The easiest way to identify hazards prior to starting a project is to break the project's plans into steps or tasks. For each task, identify any associated hazards and then decide how to eliminate or lessen them. This process is known as hazard analysis (HA); see the example in Table 3.2. The process does not have to be as formal as putting pencil to paper, although this method can be useful. The main idea is to *stop* and to *think* through all the steps to identify where potential hazards lie and to decide how to safeguard against them.

TABLE 3.2. Hazard-Analysis Example

Example: Clear the leaves from the gutters on the roof.

STEP	POTENTIAL HAZARDS	HAZARD ELIMINATION/PROTECTION
1. Grab the extension ladder from the garage and bring it to the roof.	• Poor condition of ladder • Carrying and putting the ladder into position against the house	• Inspect the ladder prior to use to make sure it is working properly. • Clear the pathway on which you plan to walk. • Use good lifting and carrying techniques. • Identify electrical power lines and other overhead hazards. • Set the ladder on a stable, level spot and at the proper angle to prevent the ladder from sliding and kicking-out.
2. Clean the leaves out of the gutters.	• Climbing on the roof • Removing leaves by hand	• Check condition of the roof for debris and secure footing. • Consider fall hazard—tie off to anchorage point on roof or work in a stable body position. • Wear proper gloves to protect hands from cuts and sharp edges.

Controlling Hazards

The best way to approach hazard control is via hazard elimination. Always strive to eliminate the hazard before moving on to other options. Three means of controlling hazards are commonly used, and the hierarchy or preference for the use of these controls is as follows:

1. Engineering controls: the use of

An electric sander equipped with a vacuum dust collector may eliminate the need to wear a dust mask.

a mechanical device to remove or significantly lessen the risk of exposure to the hazard. For example, while painting the bathroom, open a window and use a fan to pull the harmful paint vapors outside. Other examples include use of equipment guards to keep fingers away from blades, a ground fault circuit interrupter (GFCI) for electrical cords to prevent electrical shock, or an interlock control bar on a lawn mower that stops the engine when you take your hand off the handle.

2. Administrative controls: any form of nonphysical control to eliminate or to lessen exposure. An example may be the substitution of a cleaner that is low in toxicity for a fairly toxic chemical cleaner.

3. Personal protective equipment (PPE) controls: the use of safety glasses, earplugs, gloves, work boots, body coverings, a respirator, and so forth. This type of control is least preferred, as it allows the hazard to come into direct (or nearly direct) contact with the body. It is often referred to as the "last line of defense" for controlling a hazard.

Project Planning

Planning is the essence of the HA process. Regardless of how big or small the activity, proper planning ensures a good safety outcome. For instance, a common source of injury comes from the use of the wrong tool for an application due to poor planning, laziness, or lack of knowledge. What happens when you try to use a screwdriver as a chisel? How about a wrench as a hammer? When tools are not used for their intended purposes, accidents may result. Do not substitute tools or equipment for the sake of saving time or to compensate for poor planning. An example of thoughtful planning that incorpo-rates an evaluation of risk might be the following: Your task is to spend several hours cutting upper branches from trees in your yard. To complete the task you could either use an extension ladder, which would require you to make sure the ladder is stable each time you reposition it and climb the ladder with a saw in your hand to complete the work, or you could borrow or rent a ten-foot-long pole saw that allows you to work from the ground. The pole saw is a much safer option given the degree of risk involved from falling with a saw in your hand.

Recommended Practices

☑ The time immediately following a near hit or accident is the right time for reflection. Ask yourself what the root cause was for the "almost accident" that just happened and how you can prevent it from happening again. Complete the fix immediately, if possible, or at least write it down to address it later (and to avoid forgetting about the needed adjustment). To get to the root cause of a near accident, ask yourself whether the primary cause was an unsafe behavior or an unsafe condition.

☑ Always strive to eliminate a hazard using an engineering control rather than relying on PPE. Hazard elimination is always preferred over exposure minimization.

☑ Take the time in advance to plan to do the job correctly, and safety will most certainly follow. Follow the HA process described above as a safety planning tool.

☑ Identify hazards with signs, tags, and markings and always put safety first. Place a strip of masking tape on every power tool case and write "Safety First" on each as a reminder to slow down and think of the ABCs of safety. In the world of construction, many workers tape photos of their families inside their hardhats. When they're on breaks, they take their hardhats off and are reminded why they need to be committed to safety.

RESOURCES

The National Safety Council (NSC) offers off-the-job safety information on how to better understand the hazards of a home environment and improve hazard-recognition skills at http://www.nsc.org.

To purchase hazard signs or tags, visit J. J. Keller & Associates at http://www.jjkeller.com.

I post current home-safety articles and information on my website at http://www.danshomesafety.com.

Man dies after fall from roof

A 55-year-old Hilltop man was found dead today after he apparently fell off the roof of a Valleyview house where he was working. [The man] was last seen alive Tuesday night, trying to clear an animal nest out of the house's chimney, sheriff's office investigators said.

— *Columbus Dispatch*, 6 April 2011, Columbus, Ohio

A fall from as high as only three feet can result in a serious injury or even death. Falls account for 28 percent of severe injuries and deaths at home,[1] due to homeowners' using ladders improperly, falling down flights of stairs, falling off roofs, or just tripping over items around the home. Unintentional falls are the leading cause of injury in the home, resulting in 9 million emergency room visits annually.[2] See Chapter 13, "Working and Playing in the Yard," for discussion regarding head trauma following falls.

Consider the task of changing a lightbulb while you stand on a chair.

[1] National Safety Council, "Injury Facts," 2010.
[2] Centers for Disease Control and Prevention, 2009.

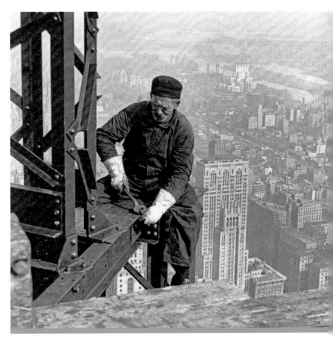

We've come a long way from accepting this type of fall hazard in the workplace. What fall hazard are you accepting at home? (Photo courtesy of Lewis Wickes Hine)

This may seem like a relatively safe chore until you acknowledge that a chair can have a fairly slippery surface, especially when it is polished and you are wearing socks. The act of stepping onto or off the chair's seat, which is at a greater height than a typical step or rung on a ladder, requires greater mental focus. A chair's stability is completely different when you stand on it versus when you sit on it. When you consider those elements, the simple activity of changing a lightbulb poses greater hazards and risk than you might have thought. After all, a chair was designed for seating, and accident prevention starts with using the correct tool for the task. Don't use a chair, box, or bucket when a ladder is needed. Let's take a look at some of the common areas where falls occur in the home and how to prevent them.

Roof Safety

The first thing you should ask yourself is, "Do I really need to go up on my roof?" If you believe the roof is damaged, you need to perform maintenance on it, or you want to install a satellite dish, hire a professional to complete the work. Don't pass the hazard on to a nonqualified person, such as your twelve-year-old neighbor. The greatest challenge when working on a roof is maintaining your balance. The steeper the angle or pitch of the roof, the more difficult it is to keep your footing. If after reading this section you feel it would be worthwhile to install a climbing-assistance or fall-protection system on your home to allow safer access to the roof, seek advice and help from a professional building contractor. Contractors use fall-protection systems on a regular basis and can provide you with specific solutions appropriate for your home. If you must go on the roof, observe the following precautions:

- Use your ladder properly to access the roof (see the next section on ladder safety).
- Wet or worn roofs (lacking granular rock) can be very slippery. Wear shoes or boots with good tread and do not climb on the roof if it is wet. Be cautious around debris, such as leaves or sticks, that could cause you to slip or trip. Dew or frost may be found on the roof in the morning and pose slippery conditions.
- Stay as far away from the edges of the roof as possible, including the gable ends of the house. A sudden loss of balance could result in a fall.
- Watch for overhead electrical hazards and stay at least ten feet away from live power lines. Although your body may not be able to reach the power line, be mindful of poles or other tools you may be using, such as a rake, that could contact the power line when extended above your head.

Worn shingles, water, and debris can create slippery roof conditions.

- Maintain a low center of gravity when you're on the roof by not standing; preferably, you should crawl or scoot on your butt to move around.
- Think of installing a device that prevents debris from accumulating in your gutters. If you routinely clean out your gutters, you risk falling off your ladder or off the roof. A gutter device is a form of engineering control that eliminates the need for working from a ladder or getting up on the roof in the first place.
- Do not tie a rope around your chimney, ventilation pipe, or any other roof object to assist you with climbing or for fall protection. It likely would not be sturdy enough

A professionally installed roof-anchorage point.

A slide guard used for roof maintenance and repair projects.

A guardrail system can even be used for a tree house!

to serve as a point to anchor. Do not purchase your own rope and hardware to design your own climbing or fall-protection system. If you are interested in installing fall-protection systems, seek professional assistance from a qualified roofing or general contractor. Fall-protection devices and protective equipment must be properly selected, installed, and used to provide adequate safety.

- Consider installing slide guards for lengthier projects, such as reshingling the roof. These are basically two-by-four-inch pieces of lumber tipped on end and anchored to the roof for the purpose of preventing you from sliding off. Contact your local building material supplier to purchase the hardware and hire a local professional to assist you with the installation.

- Investigate having a professional contractor design and install a guardrail system on your home. Guardrail systems are often used to prevent falls from decks, porches, and other elevated areas. They are commonly constructed of wood or metal and meet local or state building codes that specify the height, breaking strength, and other engineering design requirements.

Ladder Safety

Ladders are available in a variety of configurations and lengths to tackle just about any job out of the homeowner's reach. They can be constructed of wood, aluminum, fiberglass, or plastic. As with any tool, it is important to have the correct ladder for the job. Working from a ladder that is too short causes you to overreach, resulting in instability and likely a fall. Working on an aluminum ladder around electricity increases your chance of being electrocuted. Choose a ladder made from nonconducting material, such as fiberglass or wood, when working around electricity. Ladders should be used for their intended purposes and according to manufacturer's recommendations. For instance, in most cases, an extension ladder is not to be used as a plank for makeshift scaffolding or a ramp for loading your motorcycle.

All ladders are rated based on the total amount of weight they can support, which includes the weight of the user, tools, and materials they are carrying. This number is known as the ladder's capacity, and information about the capacity is commonly found on a sticker or label on the side rail of the ladder. Additionally, even though you may own a stepladder that

Read the ladder's label to find its capacity rating and other safety information.

is eight feet tall, the manufacturer will specify the top working height as either a rung position (for example, climb no higher than the second rung from the top) or its overall height. This means that your eight-foot step-ladder may only have a safe working height of six feet. It is important that you read the labels on the ladder or the instruction booklet for additional safety information. For instance, many ladder manufacturers prohibit

brace/locking mechanism

rungs

the use of modifying the ladder, such as by screwing a bucket to the ladder to hold your tools. Any add-on devices must be approved by or purchased from the manufacturer.

Let's look at the two most common types of ladders used around the home and safe practices that go along with them.

A **stepladder** is a self-support-ing ladder that is commonly found in heights ranging from four to ten feet. It is meant to be used only in its open position, with the metal locking braces (spreaders) fully engaged. A stepladder leaned against a wall in its folded or collapsed position is unsafe. It is not being used for its intended purpose if the feet of the ladder do not make contact with the ground.

Consider the following safety rec-ommendations when using steplad-ders:

- Before each use, check the con-dition of the ladder for signs of cracks, broken welds, or broken rungs (steps). If a rung is broken, do not attempt to fix or replace it. Manufacturers often require that you send the ladder to an autho-rized repair facility to be fixed.
- Make sure the locking brace mech-anisms are working freely and are in the locked position when the ladder is open and in use.

- Try to maintain at least three points of contact (two arms and a leg or two legs and an arm) when climbing, descending, or working from a ladder. Always climb or descend facing the ladder.
- Always make sure the feet or cleats of the ladder are firmly set on the surface and the ladder is level.
- Never step on the top step of a stepladder.
- Only access or climb the ladder on the rung or step side of the ladder, not the bracing side. If your work requires two people to work off the same ladder, purchase a ladder designed specifically for that purpose.
- Never lean beyond your center of balance to reach the work—move the ladder or get a taller one. The rule of thumb is to keep your bellybutton between the rails of the ladder.
- Do not attempt to balance supplies and tools on the top step. This can be hazardous to those working below. Use only the manufacturer's add-on devices (accessories), such as trays or baskets, to help with this problem. Do *not* drill holes or otherwise modify your ladder to attach your own equipment.

This ladder is specifically designed to accommodate two people working on it at one time.

Purchase the manufacturer's add-on devices rather than making your own.

An **extension ladder** must be leaned against a building or wall to be supported. It has two parallel sections that slide along each other to nearly double its length when fully

extended. Most extension ladders are made of aluminum to keep the overall weight of the ladder to a minimum, but those designed to extend to thirty feet or more can be quite heavy. To extend this type of ladder, a pulley and rope are used to slide the upper section along the inside of the lower section.

To set the ladder at the desired height, a pair of locking mechanisms grabs each rung of the lower section as it is raised. Before climbing the ladder, make sure these couplers are working freely and both mechanisms on either side of the rung are engaged.

Consider the following recommendations when using an extension ladder:

A locking mechanism

- Maintain a distance of at least ten feet from any overhead live power lines. Never use a metal ladder around sources of electricity.
- Never use the upper section of a ladder by itself, as it lacks the cleats (feet) to ensure stable footing.
- Always make sure the feet or cleats of the ladder are firmly set on the surface and the ladder is level. If working on an uneven surface is a frequent occurrence, consider purchasing a ladder that is equipped with individual leg extensions that allow one leg to be adjusted independently of the other.
- Maintain at least three points of contact when climbing, descending, or working from the ladder. Always climb or descend while facing the ladder.
- Never extend the upper section of an extension ladder so that it leaves fewer than three rungs of overlap with the bottom section.
- Extend an extension ladder at least three feet beyond the landing (such as the roof), and, if possible, secure the ladder at the top to prevent it from tipping backward or sliding to the side. Additionally, try to secure the ladder's feet by driving them into the ground several inches to prevent "kick-out" away from the building.

This ladder is equipped with adjustable-length legs for leveling.

- Never try to move a ladder while on it by "hopping."
- Do not overreach upward or to the side. Overreaching can result in a loss of balance or sideways movement of the ladder. Try to keep your bellybutton between the ladder's side rails.
- When erecting an extension ladder, place it against the building at a four-to-one height-to-base ratio. This measurement can be approximated by leaning the ladder against the building and placing your feet on the ground at the ladder's base. From that position you should be able to reach your arms

The desired four-to-one working angle of an extension ladder

An add-on stabilizer device

out parallel with the ground and grab a rung.
- Be mindful of weather conditions, such as rain, wind, and lightning, when working with the extension ladder outdoors.

- To add stability to your extension ladder, consider using outrigger or walk-through devices. An outrigger is an attachment added to the top or base of the ladder that stabilizes and prevents the ladder from

A ladder walk-through device

swaying or sliding. It can also span a window opening. A walk-through device allows you to keep walking up over the top of the ladder onto the roof without having to step

sideways off the ladder. Only purchase and use add-on devices that have been approved by the manufacturer.

Stair Safety

Nearly everyone has fallen at least partway down a flight of stairs at some point in their lives. Common causes include moving too fast, poor lighting, tripping over something left on the stairs, forgetting where the last step is, or carrying something in your arms and losing your balance. In those instances where you tumbled (or almost tumbled) down the stairs, you were probably not holding onto the handrail. Your body is most stable when you make at least three points of contact—two feet and a hand or two hands and a foot. A handrail is most commonly required on any flight of stairs that is thirty or more inches in height or includes four or more risers. All stairs are supposed to be constructed so each step and riser are uniform in dimension—depth, width, and height. This consistency tells your brain where the next step is in space, which eliminates the need to consciously think about the act of stepping.

Good stair safety means applying the following guidelines in your home:

- Keep debris and clutter off the stairs.

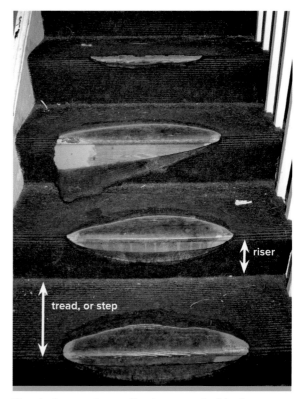

riser

tread, or step

Repair damaged carpeting to prevent a tripping hazard on the stairs.

- Make sure each flight of stairs has a firmly attached handrail.
- Use the handrail every time you go up or down the stairs.
- Make sure the stairway is well lit.
- To prevent children from tumbling down the stairs, control access to them with gates or barriers.
- Don't carry anything too large or bulky that prevents you from seeing where you are going or puts you off balance.
- Periodically check the overall condition of the stairs for loose boards or damaged carpeting.

Slips and Trips

Few things are worse than an unexpected fall in your home: Tripping on a small toy left in the hallway while you're en route to the bathroom at 2:00 AM, slipping on water puddled outside the shower door—a slip or trip can easily result in muscle strain, a broken bone, or even death. Elderly people are most vulnerable to injuries from a fall, especially those over the age of sixty-five.

Friction Is the Key!

It is pretty difficult to open a sealed jar of food with wet hands. To improve your grip, you may grab a towel, rubber pot holder, or something else to increase your leverage by creating friction against the jar's surface. The anatomy of a slip involves a part of your body, usually a hand or foot, losing traction with the surface it is trying to make contact with. This trac-  tion is caused by the friction between two objects when they come into contact—your hand and a railing, for example, or your foot and the floor. The greater the amount of friction, the less chance there is for slippage. Safety professionals spend a lot of time evaluating the slip potential of a shoe or hand with a floor, stair step, handrail, machine lever, and so forth. For high-traffic areas that are prone to collecting water, such as an outside entrance, mats or other floor coverings will help decrease the area's slip potential. A textured surface often helps with traction control. Adding texture with the use of non-skid tape or even a painted coating embedded with granular grit can help greatly. With all wear surfaces, keep in mind that replacement or repair will likely be required in time as the surface thins and becomes slippery again. Finally, watch those polishes and waxes. Shiny floors and rails look nice, but they may create a hazardous condition.. The following substances can contribute to a slippery surface:

- water
- oil and grease
- ice
- sweat
- finishes, such as wax or polish
- sand or dust

Keep the following in mind when combating slippery surfaces:

- Check the soles of your shoes for tread wear and softness of the rubber, and wear the correct glove or shoe for the job. Good shoes and gloves can make a big difference in traction control. For instance, a good leather glove works well in dry conditions, while in most cases a rubber-type glove affords

The use of slip-resistant rubber backing material helps throw rugs grip wood, laminate, and other floor surfaces.

better gripping friction in wet conditions.

- Remove throw rugs that may shift or move when stepped on, or apply a rubber backing material to the rug to hold it firmly in place.
- To assist the elederly, consider installing hand railings in all areas where sitting or lying is part of the

Nonskid tape can be easily applied to bare treads on stairs, entrance thresholds, or other high-traffic areas to help control slipping inside and outside the home.

Hand rails can be used to prevent falls around areas where sitting and standing activities take place. (Photo courtesy of Smart and Sustainable Home, Department of Housing, State of Queensland)

daily routine, such as around the toilet, bathtub, or shower. Consider installing an electric stair lift to enable elderly people to go up or down stairs more easily with minimal risk of falling. Finally, encourage the use of canes or walkers, or provide personal assistance when needed.

- Keep surfaces free from oil, grease, dust, and any other material that may cause a slip to occur.
- Keep pathways well lit and free from clutter.
- Consider applying floor coverings or coatings where slippery conditions often occur.

Falling Objects

It may not be your own fall that causes you to get hurt but rather a falling object that hits you. Take a look at storage areas around your home, such as closets or garage shelving. Are boxes, coolers, or other stacked objects teetering and ready to fall? If you have children, falling objects from above (from their perspective) may be at your waist level, so check all shelves carefully. Secure with straps or screws any heavy items that can be pulled on top of a child. In the case of an upper-level window,

the falling object may be your child. Install guards on windows above the first floor and don't rely on screens to prevent a child from falling through a window. Consider the following recommendations to prevent falling objects:

- Relocate heavy items to a lower level.
- Look at the orientation and position of stocked items. Are they stable and stacked from largest to smallest, forming a pyramid shape?

- Do not overload shelving with too many heavy items.
- When retrieving items from above your head on a shelf, stand on a ladder to put yourself at the same level as the object.
- Secure items above shoulder height using rope, straps, nets, or other means.

Recommended Practices

☑ Don't climb on your roof unless you absolutely have to. Hire a professional to complete repairs or install equipment. If you must go on the roof, consider the use of fall-protection equipment.

☑ Use ladders according to the manufacturer's instructions, and select the appropriate ladder for the project, being mindful of electrical hazards, needed working height, and other demands.

☑ Inspect ladders prior to use for signs of wear, such as a cracked or broken frame, steps, locking mechanism on a stepladder, or locking cleats on an extension ladder. If you find damage, do not attempt to fix it yourself; have it repaired by the manufacturer or a qualified repair person.

Examine storage areas for stacking stability to prevent an object from falling.

Use cords or straps to secure items that can easily fall.

✓ Place all ladders on stable, level surfaces; be mindful of doors opening into a ladder and people walking beneath or around the ladder. Where a door could swing into the ladder, lock the door and make sure only you can open it or post a sign to warn people of the ladder's presence.

✓ Inspect stairways and other areas periodically where slips and trips can result in falls. Use devices and materials that improve traction between your feet and hands and any touchable surfaces. Limit access to stairs with gates/barriers or by locking doors.

✓ Inspect areas where falling objects pose a hazard, including closets and storage shelving.

✓ If you have children, consider installing window guards on windows above the first floor to prevent anyone from falling out of the window. Do not rely on window screens to prevent a fall from a window.

Proactive Safety

Consider the inspections on the next page on a regular basis to prevent accidents and injuries from occurring.
   Note: There is a Master Inspection Schedule in the back of the book that provides recommended inspection items and frequencies. It can be found on page 157.

RESOURCES

For additional ladder safety and accessory information, visit Werner at http://www.werner ladder.com.

I post current home-safety articles and information on my website at http://www.danshomesafety .com.

Fall-Hazard Inspection Checklist

Item	Condition		Action		Date
	OK ✓	NOT OK ✗	REPAIR ✓	REPLACE ✗	
Roofs					
If you do climb on your roof, is the roof free from debris that could add to the slip or trip potential?					
If fall-protection systems are in place (guardrail, anchorage point), are they in good working condition?					
Ladders					
Are ladders (step and extension) free from cracks, dents, or other signs of wear?					
Are all the components (cleats, bracing, steps, etc.) in good condition and working properly?					
Stairways					
Are handrails present and secure?					
Are stairways sufficiently lit and free from debris, and are the treads in good condition?					
Slips and trips					
Are outside thresholds or other areas where water can exist sufficiently protected with mats, rugs, or nonstick materials?					
Are common walking areas sufficiently lit?					
Falling objects					
Are materials stored in elevated locations stacked in a stable way?					
Are stacked items secured with ropes or straps?					

Electrical Hazards

3 people electrocuted at San Bernardino home

SAN BERNARDINO, Calif. (AP) — A downed power line electrocuted a man outside his Southern California home on Friday and then killed his wife and son as they each attempted rescue in the family's backyard, authorities said.

— Amy Taxin, Associated Press, 14 January 2011

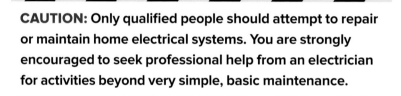

CAUTION: Only qualified people should attempt to repair or maintain home electrical systems. You are strongly encouraged to seek professional help from an electrician for activities beyond very simple, basic maintenance.

Electricity Basics

To recognize and control electrical hazards, you must have a basic understanding of how electricity works. Electricity is an incredible tool that makes nearly all aspects of daily life possible. As with so many household hazards, electricity poses the greatest threat when homeowners become complacent. It is particularly hazardous because you cannot see it, smell it, or otherwise know it is there until it is too late. Working safely with electricity means always assuming it is present until you have taken proper steps to know for certain it is not.

The best way to understand how electricity works is to think of water flowing through a pipe. The water represents electricity, and the water pipe is the wire that delivers the electricity. Like a faucet controlling water through a spout, a light switch controls the flow of electricity to the light. On the other hand, an outlet possesses no control switch. Electricity is always there, waiting to flow from the outlet into the appliance that plugs into it. The volume of electricity (how much water is moving through the pipe) is described in units of measure called *amperes*. Electricity is also described by its pressure (how hard the water is moving through the pipe), which is known as *volts*. The measurement for the amount of work electricity does, such as illuminating a lightbulb, is measured in *watts*. For example, a 60-watt lightbulb performs half the work of a 120-watt lightbulb. Electricity moving through a wire to one or more switches, lights, or outlets is called a *circuit*. A typical circuit is one that operates at 110 volts and 15 amperes. A series of circuits—usually found in walls, under floors, or in ceilings—distributes electricity throughout your home. Amperes are the greatest cause of concern, because the volume of the electricity is what stops your heart. In fact, exposure to less than 1 ampere can result in electrocution (death). A common toaster can require as many as 10 amperes to operate!

The amount of electricity needed to power your lights, appliances, DVD player, and other devices is different than the amount needed to power your telephone lines. Phone lines rely on low voltage power, and, although they may be considerably safer than your primary home electrical service, they should still be handled as if they were running on 110-volt circuits. If you have any questions about your home's electrical system, consult an electrician.

A utility company in your area is responsible for delivering electricity to your home through overhead or buried high-voltage electrical cables. If your power should go out as a result of severe weather or for some other reason, contact your utility company. *Never approach a downed power line.*

A meter located inside or outside the home measures your electrical usage and routes electricity into the home to a metal electrical panel box.

Like water flowing from a faucet, electricity moves through the wire to switches, outlets, and appliances.

A common electric meter

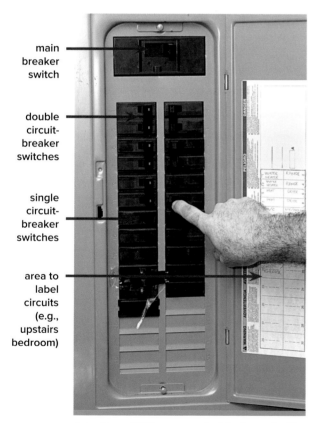

main breaker switch

double circuit-breaker switches

single circuit-breaker switches

area to label circuits (e.g., upstairs bedroom)

A common 200-ampere electrical panel with circuit-breaker switches

The electrical panel allows for the distribution of electricity and controls each circuit in the home through a device called a circuit breaker or fuse. A fuse or circuit breaker is a safety device that is engineered to allow a specified maximum amount of electricity to flow through it; it fails safe, or "trips open," to interrupt the circuit when the demand for electricity in the circuit is too high. The breaker may trip, or shut the circuit off, when you plug too many appliances into one circuit—demanding more amperes than the circuit (wire) is designed to carry. Each circuit breaker will typically serve one area or room in the house and should be labeled in your breaker box as "main floor bathroom," "basement outlets," and so forth. Electricity for an entire circuit can be controlled at the electrical panel simply by flipping off the appropriate circuit breaker or removing the fuse. The "main" circuit breaker interrupts electrical power to all the individual circuit breakers in the box, thus turning off all power in the home. *Warning*: Although the main breaker switch can be turned off or closed, the primary electrical cable delivering power to the panel is still live or "hot" with electricity. Certain parts of the panel board carry electricity at all times and therefore require extreme caution. When a breaker or fuse fails, replace it with only the properly rated breaker for that circuit. *Never* insert a 20-ampere breaker into a 15 ampere-rated circuit. This can overload the wires and cause damage or possibly a fire.

Remember, a circuit breaker or fuse is designed to protect the electrical system and the appliances that connect to it—not you! Other devices discussed later in this chapter are designed to protect people from electrocution.

Wires and Cords

The circuits in your home consist of wires running through walls, floors, and ceilings. An extension cord is a temporary wire allowing electricity to be delivered from an outlet to a tool or appliance. An extension cord should never be used to permanently deliver electricity.

A wire or cord is designed to carry up to a specific maximum amount of electricity. This amount is referred to as the wire's rating, or *gauge*. The gauge refers to the thickness, or diameter, of the wire. Generally speaking, the thicker the wire (the smaller the gauge number), the more electricity it can safely transmit. A 15-ampere-rated wire is designed to carry no more than 15 amperes of electricity. However, a wire or cord does not know how much electricity it is supposed to carry and will try to deliver as much as the appliance needs. As electricity flows through a

circuit's wire, some of the electrical energy is lost in the form of heat, causing your appliance or extension cords to become warm and more flexible during use. Too much of an electrical supply on a cord results in the buildup of heat, causing failure and resulting in a fire. Overloading a wire with too much electricity causes damage to the wire. Scorch marks on outlet covers are a typical sign of an overload to a circuit. When a circuit is overloaded, homeowners typically rely on the circuit breaker or fuse to work properly by shutting down the

During construction, an electrical wire runs through a wall and enters a switch box to provide power to ceiling lights.

flow of electricity. It is not a safe practice to rely on the electrical system safety features, as these will fail in time if continually abused.

To be proactive and prevent overloading a circuit, you need to know

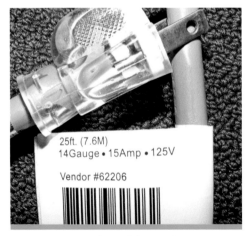

The gauge, or rating, of the cord

how much electricity your circuit will tolerate and determine how much electricity is being serviced by the circuit. This can be accomplished simply by adding the total electrical demand for each appliance plugged into the circuit, assuming that everything is turned on at the same time. For example, a circuit that serves your living room is 15 amperes and has all of the following plugged into it: a TV (5 amperes), a stereo (3 amperes), and table and ceiling lights (3 amperes). Assume all are on. This totals 11 amperes, an amount that is well within the safe operating range of the 15-ampere wire and circuit. What happens when you plug the 12-ampere vacuum cleaner into the wall outlet served by the same circuit? Your total now exceeds 15 amperes, so you blow the breaker! Having this happen time and time again places a strain on your electrical system and in time will cause it to fail.

A rating system has been developed to provide the user with an understanding of the cord's recommended uses and limitations. These ratings, consisting of a series of letters, are commonly understood by electricians and are better described to the consumer with directions found on the product packaging, such as, "For indoor use only." The rating of an extension cord or appliance cord tells you its safe operating limits and can usually be found on the covering of the cord or on a tag near the plug. For outdoor applications, use cords and devices that are approved for outside use and that are described as being "heavy duty" or "contractor grade." Extension cords rated "SJTW" or "SJEOW" may be used for portable tools and equipment, portable appliances, small motors, and associated machinery. These portable cords have excellent resistance to oil and moisture, good tensile strength, high flexibility, and excellent abrasion resistance. A "SOW"-rated cord is water resistant.

Extension cords can receive substantial abuse. Inspect cords frequently for cuts, gouges, pinched areas, and so forth. Running your hand slowly over the entire length of the cord will help you find cuts or damage to the outer casing. A "fix" with duct tape or electrical tape is really not a fix. If the cord shows obvious damage, replace it rather than attempting to repair it and destroy the old cord to prevent future use. Lastly, use an extension cord for its intended purpose, and never use it as a piece of rope.

This vacuum cord has developed a break in the outer casing. Replacing the cord is recommended.

Power Strips or Outlet Adapters

Power strips or outlet adapters are often misused. Their intended purpose is to make additional outlets available while occupying only a single wall

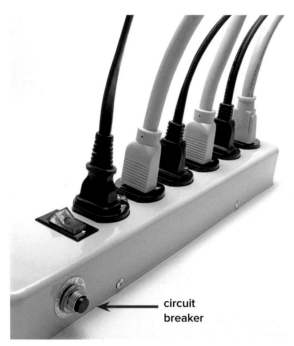

circuit
breaker

outlet. Power strips are commonly used behind entertainment systems where outlets are limited and many electrical devices, such as a VCR, DVD player, gaming system, TV, and audio receiver, need power. However, power strips are frequently overloaded. The sum of all items plugged into it should not exceed the power strip rating. For example a 15-ampere circuit powering a 15-ampere-rated power strip/adapter cannot accommodate more than 15 total amperes of electrical demand. Overload can cause failure and fire. Some of the more expensive power strips have built-in circuit breakers or fuses that prevent an overload from occurring. Check the rating on any power strip you use, as many are recommended for indoor use only.

Ground Fault Circuit Interrupter

The ground fault circuit interrupter (GFCI) is a device that helps prevent electrical shock. It senses a surge or a sudden demand for electricity, which can be caused by a short (cut wire) or when your body touches an unprotected (bare) electrical wire. In a fraction of a second, the GFCI

stops the flow of electricity through the wire (and through you!). It can be a portable device or a feature found on an outlet. Its use is strongly recommended for all outside electrical activities. Electrical code requires GFCI-protected outlets near supplies of water, such as the bathroom or kitchen. If your home outlets near water are not protected by a GFCI device, contact a qualified electrician to discuss your options.

A GFCI outlet includes "test" and "reset" buttons to test its working condition. A GFCI should be tested at least twice per year, because, like any other mechanical devices, it can fail. To test a GFCI, plug an item, such as a radio, into the outlet, turn on the radio, and then push the "test" button, which opens the circuit and simulates a short. If the GFCI is working properly, the radio should turn off. If the GFCI is not working properly, call an electrician to replace it. When you're finished with the test, press the "reset" button. Some homes may be equipped with a GFCI system at the electrical panel that protects all the circuits in the home at all locations—switches, outlets, and receptacles.

A portable GFCI should be plugged into the outlet or closest to the electrical source that needs protection. An extension cord plugged into a GFCI that is itself plugged into the outlet protects the entire cord and anything plugged into it. Like other electrical hardware, GFCIs are rated for specific amperage. The outlet, GFCI, extension cord, and electrical device all have to be rated for an equal number of amperes.

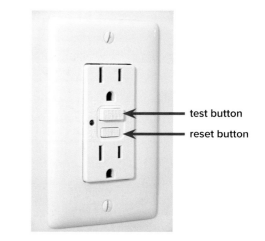

test button
reset button

A GFCI wall outlet with "test" and "reset" buttons

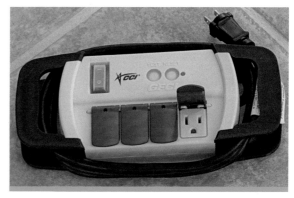

A portable multioutlet GFCI protector

A GFCI plug that plugs directly into an outlet to protect it

Design and Codes

Nearly all cords, wires, and electrical devices manufactured in the United States have been designed for safe operating use. To ensure that minimum safety performance standards have been met, electrical equipment is tested by testing services. The most common design testing service is that provided by Underwriters Laboratory (UL), a highly respected independent testing laboratory. A UL-listed device is one that has been rigorously tested to meet certain electrical performance standards intended to reduce the chance of electrical shock and fire. Look for the UL logo on cords and appliances to ensure that they meet UL standards. The UL listing may also be found in the operations manual or on the manufacturer's tag on the device.

The Underwriters Laboratory logo

Electrical codes are the rules building professionals, such as electricians, are required to follow to ensure electrical safety. National and local codes require the use of certain safety devices, such as GFCIs, circuit breakers, and rated wires. Codes help prevent electrical injury and fires. The National Electrical Code (NEC) establishes the minimum safety design standards for electrical systems in the United States. Many cities have additional electrical code requirements that an electrician or homeowner must be aware of when making repairs. Knowing and observing these code requirements for all home repairs will help you make your home as safe as possible.

Working Safely

The key to working with electricity safely is control: You must control when and how electricity is delivered to a device and throughout the home. To ensure that you will not be electrocuted, turn the circuit off or unplug the device that you are working on before beginning work. Whether you are removing something that got stuck in a vacuum cleaner or trying to remove a broken lightbulb from a light fixture, *turn the power supply off*. For the vacuum cleaner, it is as simple as unplugging it from the wall outlet.

For the broken lightbulb, find the corresponding circuit breaker in the electrical panel and flip the breaker switch to the "off" position to cut off power to the circuit. Wouldn't turning off the light switch be an easier way to turn off the light fixture? Yes. Does doing so provide the greatest level of safety? No. What happens if you get off your ladder to grab a tool and your child or spouse comes into the room and turns on the light switch without your knowing about it? Go the extra mile to completely cut off power to the circuit by flipping the breaker switch to the "off" position. When you do this, let others in the house know what you are doing, as other devices are likely run by the same circuit.

Find the Power!

A current tester allows you to determine whether electricity is flowing to a source, such as an outlet. The device provides an extra level of certainty that you have properly cut off power to the circuit you are working on. Some makes and models are designed to light up or to "chirp" audibly when inserted into an outlet where electricity is present. Read the instructions carefully to ensure proper use of these devices.

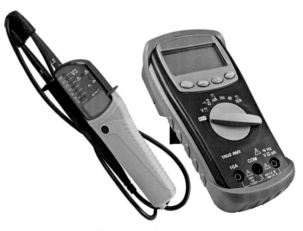

Current-testing devices

ground pin

Grounding is the process by which stray electrical current that is present in an appliance or cord is safely discharged, preventing electrical shock. A grounded three-prong plug paired with a three-hole outlet achieves grounding through the dedicated third prong.

Never alter the grounding capability of a plug or cord. For instance, never turn a three-prong plug into a two-prong plug to make it fit into an outlet. Where possible, use three-prong extension cords as well.

A polarized plug includes one prong that is wider than the other. Polarized outlets prevent a plug being inserted in a way that can cause an electrically unsafe condition.

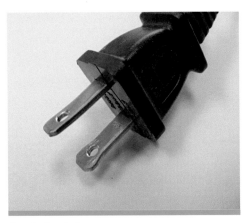

A polarized plug

To prevent children from sticking fingers or objects into outlets, consider covering unused outlets with plastic inserts. These inserts require considerable force to remove and provide a reasonable level of safety.

Recommended Practices

Protective cap inserts

☑ Understand your home electrical system, starting at the electrical service panel. Know which breakers or fuses control which circuits and the ampere rating for each.

☑ Determine the circuit's maximum capacity—usually 15 or 20 amperes—and add up the entire operating amperage total for each circuit to make sure no more than that amount of electricity is being drawn through the circuit. Be mindful that a circuit can include ceiling lights. Overloading the circuit and merely relying on the circuit breaker to trip is not safety smart and could result in damage to the wiring system and possibly a fire.

☑ Before sinking nails or screws into walls, floors, or ceilings, know where your electrical wires are located. This may require the assistance of an electrician who has access to devices to determine the location of circuit wire.

☑ Inspect outlets and receptacles for damage, such as scorch marks or broken/missing cover plates.

☑ Turn off the electricity flowing to any part of the system that you need to work on by unplugging the device or turning off the corresponding circuit breaker. Avoid turning off an object simply by turning off the breaker. If you do not unplug the device or turn its power switch off, you may have an unwanted startup of the device when you turn the breaker switch back on.

☑ To determine whether an outlet is still energized, or "hot," use a tester. Additionally, some extension cords ends are made of clear plastic that is designed to "glow" at the receptacle end to indicate the presence of electricity.

☑ Test GFCIs at least twice a year.

☑ After you have unplugged a device, inspect power strips and extension cords for damage, missing ground pins, cuts, and exposed wires. Slowly run your hand over a cord to feel for cuts in the outer casing.

☑ For any repairs, contact a qualified electrician.

☑ Use GFCI devices outdoors and inside where water is present or overloading the circuit is probable.

☑ *Always* assume that an electrical circuit is live until you have turned off the power.

Proactive Safety

The following items should be inspected frequently to ensure proper working condition.

Electrical Safety Inspection Checklist

ITEM	CONDITION		ACTION		DATE
	OK ✔	NOT OK ✘	REPAIR ✔	REPLACE ✘	
Panel or fuse box					
Is the panel door closed and locked to limit access?					
Do you see signs of burns, scorch marks, or a faulty breaker/fuse? If so, overload has possibly occurred—have an electrician inspect the area.					
Outlets					
Are child safety caps in place if needed?					
Do you see burn or scorch marks? If so, overload has possibly occurred—have an electrician inspect the area.					
Have you tested your GFCIs?					
Are face plates or covers installed on all outlets?					
Power strip					
Does the total appliance demand plugged into the strip not exceed the strip or circuit rating?					
Does the total appliance demand plugged into the strip not exceed the strip or circuit rating?					
If the strip is used outdoors, has it been inspected to make sure it is rated for outside use?					
Extension cords					
Do the cords exhibit cuts, gouges, pinched areas, or other damage?					

(cont'd.)

Electrical Safety Inspection Checklist (cont'd.)

Item	Condition		Action		Date
	OK ✔	NOT OK ✗	REPAIR ✔	REPLACE ✗	
Is the grounding prong in place, if equipped with one?					
Is the cord properly rated for outside use?					
Are any cords running through water? If so, immediately reroute the cord.					
Appliance and power tools					
Have they been inspected for damage or wear and tear?					

RESOURCES

 A program of the Energy Education Council, SafeElectricity.org provides additional information on home electrical safety, including compelling video testimonials of individuals injured by electricity, at http://www.safeelectricity.com.

Underwriters Laboratory (UL) provides safety information, including electrical and fire prevention, at http://www.safetyathome.com.

 For information on home electrical codes and do-it-yourself construction electrical safety, visit http://www.ask-the-electrician.com/home-electrical-codes.html.

I post current home-safety articles and information on my website at http://www.danshomesafety.com.

Chemical Hazards

Man receives chemical burns in home project

While pouring a concrete slab for a dog kennel, a Lake Elmo man received burns to his leg after wet concrete ran down inside his boot. "I had no idea that concrete could cause chemical burns," said the homeowner. The man drove himself to the emergency room, where he was treated and released. Moderate scarring of the skin will likely remain.

— Lake Elmo, MN

Children are particularly susceptible to chemical hazards in the home.

The story above is not taken from any real news outlet, but it illustrates something that happens to construction workers all the time. Hundreds of thousands of chemicals are manufactured, transported, and used in the United States each year. Only a small number make it to the home in the form of a consumer product. These household chemical products include paints, disinfectants, cleaners, pesticides, glues, beauty aids, and fertilizers. Improperly used, these products present a health risk. (*Note:* The hazards associated with fuels are covered in Chapter 7, "Fire Prevention and Preparedness.")

Your Exposure

Controlling your exposure to chemicals starts with safe handling practices.

Many commonly used cleaning products contain strong chemicals.

To understand why chemicals can cause harm, you must know how you can be exposed. Exposure is the process by which a chemical comes into contact with your body. Once on or inside the body, a chemical's effect can range from just mild skin irritation or, in the case of poisoning, death. It is estimated that a poisoning occurs every fourteen seconds in the United States. Poisoning can occur as a result of an intentional or unintentional exposure to a chemical or a medicine.

The pathway through which exposure occurs depends upon the chemical's form: liquid, aerosol, gas, or solid. People often rely on their senses to detect exposure. A foul odor, burning eyes, headache, or nausea may indicate chemical exposure. Oftentimes, chemicals contain odorants that im-

part a more-pleasant smell, but an unfortunate side effect is that they can mask exposure and provide the user with a false sense of safety. Health effects due to exposure can be immediate or delayed. Examples of products

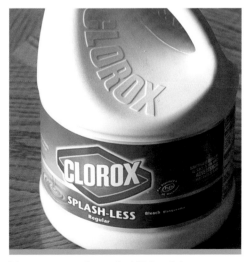

Most common household bleach has a pungent burning odor, which is a good warning property that can help prevent you from inhaling too much of it.

where immediate exposure is a concern include cleaning chemicals containing chlorine or wood stains containing highly volatile solvents. Some chemicals, such as silica dust from sanding sheetrock or cutting concrete, require years of continued exposure to result in health problems, including the debilitating respiratory illness called silicosis.

If you feel ill while using a household chemical, stop what you are doing. Exit the work area, get some fresh air, and reread the manufacturer's use instructions on the container label. You need to proactively control your exposure through engineering, administrative, or personal protective equipment (PPE) controls, which are covered in Chapter 3, "Safety Basics."

Chemical Exposure Routes

Chemicals can enter the body via inhalation, contact, and ingestion.

Inhalation: Chemicals can be breathed in through the mouth or nose.

Contact: Chemicals may sit on the skin or be absorbed through it. Contact exposure can also occur through a cut or injection via a sharp object.

Ingestion: Chemicals can enter through the mouth directly, by hand-to-mouth activity, or by eating food that has come into contact with a chemical.

Inhaling a chemical is the exposure route of greatest concern. A chemical that enters the lungs is readily absorbed into the bloodstream. Pay particular attention to this route of exposure and always use proper controls to prevent breathing in a chemical. The frequency of exposure, the concentration of the chemical, and the user's level of protection from exposure determine the overall health effect.

The Occupational Health and Safety Administration (OSHA) establishes and enforces safe levels of chemical exposure for the workplace. In the home, no such limits exist, so you must protect yourself against chemical exposures.

For household chemicals, exposure control through hazard recognition starts with product selection. Understand what you buy. Read the container labels and pay attention to

TABLE 6.2. Cleaning Products

Chemical Type	Example	Exposure Pathway	Primary Short-Term Health Effect
Corrosive (acid)	Soap-scum cleaner	Contact, inhalation	Irritation to the skin
Corrosive (base)	Silver-tarnish remover	Contact	Burns
Corrosive (base)	Drain cleaner (caustic soda or lye)	Contact, inhalation	Severe burns
Disinfectant	Bleach	Inhalation, contact	Burns
Disinfectant	Cleaning wipes	Contact (eye)	Irritation to the eye
Petroleum	Liquid furniture polish	Ingestion	Nausea, fatal in larger quantities
Petroleum/ammonia	Brass polish	Contact	Irritation to the eye

TABLE 6.3. Health and Beauty Products

Chemical Type	Example	Exposure Pathway	Primary Short-Term Health Effect
Alcohol/acetone	Nail-polish remover	Contact	Irritant, flammable
Flammable gases/ aerosols	Hair spray	Inhalation	Flammable
Flammable liquid	Bug repellant	Contact	Flammable
Oxidizer	Hydrogen peroxide (antiseptic)	Contact	Irritant, tissue damage

TABLE 6.4. Maintenance Products

Chemical Type	Example	Exposure Pathway	Primary Short-Term Health Effect
Alcohol (methyl, glycol)	Windshield washer fluid or antifreeze	Ingestion	Toxic even in small quantities
Fertilizer	Lawn or garden food	Inhalation, contact	Irritation to skin and respiratory system
Herbicide	Weed killer	Contact	Irritation (eyes)
Pesticide	Bug spray	Inhalation, contact	Respiratory irritation
Petroleum	Gasoline, oil, grease, lacquer thinner, charcoal starter fluid	Contact, inhalation	Flammable

warning statements regarding exposure. Common household chemical types and their related health effects are described in Tables 6.2, 6.3, and 6.4, above. For this discussion, chemical products are grouped into three major categories: cleaning products, health and beauty supplies, and maintenance products.

Sanding a solid material is a process hazard, because it creates dust.

Process Hazards

A process hazard is one in which the parent material poses no exposure threat, but during the course of using the material, an exposure is created. For instance, when you use a soldering iron for an electronic repair project, the metal solder wire may contain lead that presents little exposure in solid form, but the smoke from the soldering process can be fairly toxic. In this case, exposure can be controlled by working outside (administrative control) or using a small fan (engineering control) to blow across the work to push the harmful fumes away. Alternatively consider using a nonlead solder (administrative control) or a respirator (PPE control).

Another example of a process hazard is a sanding activity involving metal, wood, or cement. The solid material may not be particularly toxic, but the dust generated from the sanding activity poses a hazard. In these examples, exposure to metal dust, pesticides contained in chemically treated ("green") wood, and silica need to be controlled. Use the principles of completing the hazard analysis, found in Chapter 3, "Safety Basics," to pinpoint where you may be at risk of exposure.

Labels and Use

Federal regulations, including the Toxic Substance Control Act and those set forth by the Consumer Product Safety Commission, require manufacturers to include safety information for chemical-based products. The information—usually found on a label or insert in the packaging—includes the product's chemical contents, proper use, health risks associated with exposure, and recommended safe practices. *Read this information!* Consumers get themselves into trouble when they conclude, "If a half cup is good, a full cup is better." A manufacturer's determination of safe levels of exposure to its chemical is based on the fact that you will be using the product according to the provided guidelines regarding how and where to use it, required PPE, and compatibility with other cleaning materials. If you deviate from these recommendations, you may be at a greater risk of exposure.

Every container in your home should have a label on it. How else do you know what's inside? Secondary containers are those that contain a chemical transferred from its original parent container. We often use a milk

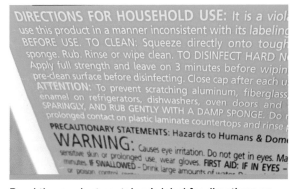

Read the product container's label for directions on use and exposure warnings.

What's inside—antifreeze, windshield-washer fluid, or liquid fertilizer?

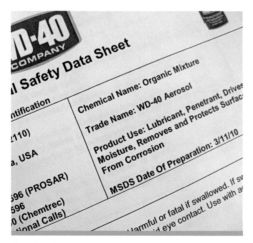

For detailed information about a chemical, obtain an MSDS by downloading one from the manufacturer's website or by calling the company that produced the chemical.

jug, pop bottle, ice cream bucket, or food canning jar to store leftovers. Write on a piece of masking tape with a permanent pen or directly on the container itself to indicate what's inside. Trying to determine the contents by sniffing is not safety smart. If you use a secondary container to hold chemical leftovers, determine the compatibility of the container with the contents. A milk jug was designed to hold milk, not gasoline. It may fail, leaving you with a big mess.

Material Safety Data Sheets

It is nearly impossible to adequately communicate on a product label all the risks a chemical poses. To completely describe the potential hazards of chemicals and chemical-based products, manufacturers are required to prepare Material Safety Data Sheets (MSDSs). These multipage documents contain information about exposure, safe handling, PPE, spill cleanup, health effects, and fire-safety recommendations. All MSDSs are available to the general public and can be requested from the manufacturers by calling them or checking their websites for printable copies. See the end of this chapter for resources on obtaining MSDS information.

Chemical Exposure Control

Various controls allow you to eliminate or lessen your hazard exposure. You owe it to yourself to continuously strive to minimize exposure at every opportunity. Being smart about controlling chemical exposure starts the same way all other hazard control does—with thinking. Follow the hazard-analysis method described in Chapter 3: Visualize and walk yourself through an activity from start to finish, determining where your risk of exposure lies and how to eliminate it.

Consider the example of applying a dry fertilizer or herbicide product to your lawn. Reading the label on the bag provides precautions about exposure, including a likely mention about avoiding direct contact. Many homeowners simply put on their grungy tennis shoes and old work jeans before loading the spreaders. Wearing anything on your feet to protect your skin from chemical contact is certainly better than going barefoot, but it is easy to forget about the need to contain the spread of the chemical. After completing the task, many homeowners simply kick their shoes off at the back door without first cleaning or decontaminating them; many others wear the same shoes the following day to complete messy projects inside the house, unknowingly allowing the chemical to enter their home. Another example may be a home renovation project where the homeowner suspects but has not confirmed the presence of lead-based paint. During the course of the renovation, dust is created that deposits on the homeowner's clothing. The clothes go into the washing machine and dryer, where the lead dust then contaminates the other clothes as well. Additionally, without controlling lead dust as recommended by the Environmental Protection Agency (EPA), the dust will enter the

Wearing sandals while applying lawn fertilizer is *not* an effective way to control chemical exposure.

ventilation system and potentially spread throughout the home.

Minimizing exposure requires planning before using the chemical. Observe the following practices for exposure control:

- Work small, manageable areas, one at a time, to exercise control over how much exposure occurs.
- When working with volatile products (such as stains or solvents), use only the amount you need and work from containers with small openings. Pouring a quart of stain into a large ice cream pail allows a lot of stain to evaporate, versus working from a smaller glass canning jar.
- Read the container label for recommended use and cleanup procedures. Don't walk through the house while wearing contaminated clothing. First, consider gross removal with a shop vac for dust or soak the garments in the utility sink or outside with a garden hose to remove the bulk of the contaminant before tossing clothing into the laundry machine. If you do use a vacuum for any dust collection, make sure it includes a high efficiency particulate air (HEPA) filter to ensure total capture of dust.
- Apply the same principle of a gross wash of your hands, face, and other areas of the body you suspect may have chemicals on them. The more contaminant you can keep outside the house, the better.

Storing Chemicals

To minimize exposure, store chemicals properly:

- Secure containers by limiting access to them. Keep them in locked cabinets and make sure that all containers have child-proof caps.
- Store containers inside plastic bins to collect spills in the event that the containers leak.
- Segregate and store "like" materials (such as all flammable liquids in one area, all corrosives in another, and so forth) to reduce the possibility of two different chemicals interacting. Mixing chemicals is usually not a good practice and can create toxic gases.
- Minimize and keep only the products that you need. The more chemicals you have on hand, the greater the danger of exposure.

Anticipate a Mishap

You should know what to do if you have an accidental spill or medical emergency involving a household chemical. Take the time to read the label or MSDS information prior to use and plan accordingly. Typical use of the product may not require PPE, but if you spill a whole gallon of cleaner, PPE may be required. Keep cleanup supplies on hand and dispose of chemicals responsibly. Simply dumping chemicals in the trash or down the drain can be dangerous. Never put yourself in harm's way in order to complete a cleanup. If the situation is beyond your control, dial 911 or your local poison control center.

Recommended Practices

☑ Remember the preferred order of hazard elimination or reduction: (1) engineering controls (such as ventilation), (2) administrative controls (such as choosing a less hazardous or toxic product), and (3) personal protective equipment (PPE, such as gloves, goggles, or respirator). Ventilate where possible, especially when working in enclosed or confined spaces, such as shower stalls, attics, crawl spaces, sheds, or other small areas.

☑ Labels—chemical manufacturers are required to place certain hazard warnings on container labels. Read and follow these warnings. If you do not understand the warnings, contact the manufacturerer's consumer hotline. Use the product according to the label recommendations. Make sure every container has a label on it (or is marked), including secondary containers.

☑ Go the extra mile to completely understand a chemical's hazards by obtaining a copy of the Material Safety Data Sheet (MSDS). A label generally only provide the basic, critical safety information, but manufacturers are required to publish detailed information about their products, information that is contained in what is called an MSDS. The manufacturer is required to furnish this information upon request, and it can usually be obtained from the manufacturer's website or by calling the manufacter directly.

☑ *Never* combine products, especially cleaning chemicals, to a make a "super product." For instance, the combination of window cleaner (containing ammonia) and bleach (containing chlorine) creates a highly toxic ammonium chloride white gas. In certain cases, chemical products can spontaneously catch fire or create corrosive and toxic gases when combined. The container label or MSDS information will usually describe the product's compatibility.

☑ Select and use PPE based on the manufacturer's recommendations, which can be found on either the container label or MSDS. More information on PPE is contained in Chapter 9, "Personal Protective Equipment."

☑ Dedicate certain clothing to messy, chemical-based work and pre-wash clothing prior to placing it in the washing machine to control the spread of chemical powders, dusts, splatters, and residues.

☑ Segregate products based on compatibility. Limit access to them and provide for spill containment.

☑ Talk to your children about the hazards associated with chemicals. Consider using easily identifiable labels, such as Mr. Yuk stickers, to mark chemical containers as "do not touch." See the Resources section at the end of this chapter for information on how to purchase these stickers and other relevant educational materials.

A Mr. Yuk sticker

☑ Dispose of chemicals responsibly and lawfully. Take advantage of your local household hazardous waste collection facilities to allow reuse or proper disposal of old chemicals. Contact your city or county government to find out about free or inexpensive disposal programs in your area. Most communities sponsor a household hazardous waste collection event to allow for proper disposal of unwanted household chemicals. Read label information about disposal options. In many cases, pouring a chemical down a sink or toilet results in harmful vapors returning through the sink, floor, or shower drain.

✓ Know the signs and symptoms of overexposure (such as burning eyes or throat irritation) and what to do if you or someone accidentally becomes overexposed. This information can usually be found on the container label or MSDS. If you need immediate medical attention, dial 911 or contact your local poison control center by dialing the national hotline (800) 222-1222.

Proactive Safety

The following checklist can be used to help prevent injury and exposure from chemicals in the home.

Chemical Exposure Safety Checklist

ITEM	CONDITION		ACTION		DATE
	OK ✓	NOT OK ✗	REPAIR ✓	REPLACE ✗	
Engineering controls					
Are you using ventilation fans or other forms of engineering controls to remove any hazard conditions from the air?					
Labels and markings					
Are all chemical containers, including secondary containers (such as a recycled milk jug), sufficiently labeled or marked to identify their contents?					
Storage					
Are your storage areas secured with locks?					
Do storage areas provide for spill containment?					
Are you prepared to deal with a spill?					
PPE					
Do you have the correct PPE for the chemicals you are using, and is it in good condition?					

RESOURCES

Contact the Association of Poison Control Centers at http://www.aapcc.org/dnn/Home.aspx or (800) 222-1222 to find the nearest poison control center.

Search for product MSDSs at http://www.msdssearch.com or http://www.ehso.com/msds.php or by calling (877) 673-7123.

A fun game for kids that helps them practice selecting and using of PPE can be found at http:// www.planet-science.com/categories /under-11s/games/2010/09/fashionable -labs.aspx.

To purchase "Mr. Yuk" stickers, labels, and related children's educational materials go to http://www.upmc.com/Services/poison center/Pages/educational-materials .aspx#stickers.

I post current home-safety articles and information on my website at http://www.danshome safety.com.

Fire Prevention and Preparedness

Fatal Christmas house fire started in kitchen

The fire that lead to the death of 67-year-old Carolyn Hoose inside her Cravey Trail home Christmas Day started in the kitchen's cooking area, the DeKalb County Fire Department said this week.

— *Northdruid Hills–Briarcliff Patch*, 30 December 2010, DeKalb, IL

In 2010 U.S. fire departments responded to *384,000 home fires.* Home fires caused 17,720 injuries, 3,120 deaths (85 percent of all fire fatalities), and $11.6 billion in property damage.[1] Fires change lives without warning, yet almost all fires are preventable. Fire kills most often by asphyxiation (lack of oxygen) due to smoke inhalation. Most home fires are related to cooking, and the leading cause of fire death is due to smoking. Almost two-thirds (63 percent) of reported home fire deaths resulted from fires in homes without working smoke alarms.[2] These statistics and those in Figures 7.1 and 7.2 on the next page provide valuable insight into the need for fire-prevention and fire-preparedness efforts.

[1] National Fire Protection Association statistics, 2010.
[2] National Fire Protection Association statistics, 2010.

How Fire Works

Fire requires a fuel source (such as gasoline, paper, or dryer lint), oxygen, and an ignition source (such as open flame, a spark, heat, or static electric-

ity). These elements are referred to as the fire triangle. For fire to occur, all three must be present in a proper proportion. For example, air must

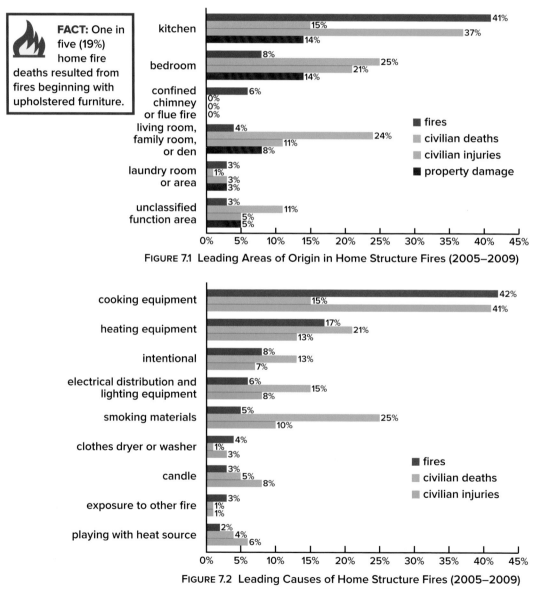

FACT: One in five (19%) home fire deaths resulted from fires beginning with upholstered furniture.

FIGURE 7.1 Leading Areas of Origin in Home Structure Fires (2005–2009)

FIGURE 7.2 Leading Causes of Home Structure Fires (2005–2009)

(Source: Marty Ahrens, "Home Structure Fires," May 2011, http://www.nfpa.org/assets/files/PDF/OS.Homes.pdf.)

contain at least 2 percent and no more than 11 percent propane gas for it to combust or burn. In this example, if you don't have enough propane gas, the fuel-air mixture is said to be too lean. If you have too much propane gas, the mixture is said to be too rich. Even when their proportions are correct, removing any one of the three fire-triangle components will extinguish the fire. A grease fire in a frying pan can be easily extinguished by putting the lid on the pan to remove the supply of oxygen. A fire extinguisher that uses carbon dioxide (CO_2) as the extinguishing agent works in a similar way by blowing CO_2 across the flame and displacing oxygen. Spraying water on a fire extinguishes the fire by removing the ignition source, the flame or heat.

The fire triangle

Fuel Sources and Prevention

Fire prevention starts with managing the handling, storage, and use of fuels and ignition sources. The largest sources of fuel in the home are oils and greases, flammable gases, and combustible and flammable liquids. Common safety concerns for each are described below:

- **Oils and greases** Forty percent of all fires take place in the kitchen, many of them attributed to cooking oils and greases. The kitchen usually provides a common source of open flame—the stove. Oils and grease can catch fire directly when in contact with an open flame or when heated to sufficient temperatures. *Do not leave food cooking in oil and grease on a stove unattended.* Oil and grease can splatter out of pans and come into direct contact with a stove's burner flame or electric coil. Dropping

Grease fires are one of the leading causes of house fires.

frozen foods into a deep fryer is also extremely dangerous, because water in the frozen item is immediately changed to steam, resulting in a near explosion. Instead, thaw all frozen foods prior to deep frying. Do *not* attempt to extinguish an oil or grease fire with water, because it merely spreads the flame. If a fire starts in a pot or pan, simply put the lid onto it or spray it with a non-water-based fire extinguisher (see "Fire Preparedness," below). Finally, regularly clean the stove where oil and grease have splattered and built up to remove potential fuel sources. Don't forget to clean the ventilation hood over the stove where grease residue can quickly build up.

Natural gas or propane appliances are clean and efficient but present a fire hazard because they use open flames.

- **Natural gas** Natural gas is a clean, energy-efficient way to heat homes and is found in all urban areas. Furnaces, water heaters, stoves, fireplaces, and clothes dryers may be powered with natural gas. Natural gas is extracted from the earth and is odorless. Your natural gas provider adds a chemical odorant called mercaptan that gives it a distinct smell similar to that of rotten eggs. Natural gas is highly flammable. If you smell natural gas and know that your stove burners are off, you likely have a leak in your system. In this case, leave your home immediately and dial 911 from a safe location, such as a neighbor's house. Do not turn off the lights or use the phone before you leave the home, because electricity can serve as an ignition source. Homes can explode violently from the buildup and ignition of natural gas. If repairs are needed, call a licensed professional. Do *not* attempt to perform work on your natural gas system unless you are properly trained.
- **Propane** Propane, also known as liquefied petroleum gas (LPG), is commonly used as a fuel source for outdoor grills and furnaces for homes in rural areas. A supply of propane used for the home is com-

monly stored in large pressure tanks located outside the home. Safe use of propane requires the proper operation of the tank/cylinder, hose or distribution line, regulator, and any connected appliance. The tank should be inspected regularly for signs of rust, dents, or other damage. If you're unsure of the tank's condition, contact your nearest propane supplier and ask for an inspection.

Tanks store the propane as a liquid under pressure. Opening the valve on the top of the tank allows some of the liquid propane to expand as a gas and travel through the hose to the appliance. The gas must first pass through the regulator to get through the hose. The regulator lowers the pressure of the gas leaving the tank. Propane delivered at a pressure level that is too high can create an unsafe condition that could result in an explosion. Inspect the hose, regulator, and valve for any obvious signs of rust, cracks, kinks, or damage. If you're unsure of the condition of these items, have a qualified propane professional complete an inspection. Finally, close the tank valve when a grill or heater is not in use to minimize the chance of accidentally releasing propane

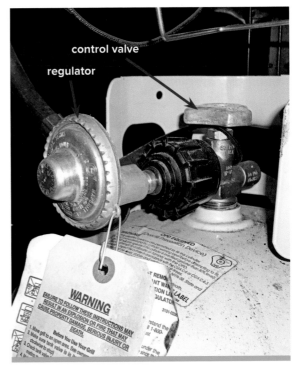

control valve

regulator

The regulator and control valve on a common propane tank for a grill

inside the grill, garage, or other enclosed area.

- **Aerosols** An aerosol is not actually a flammable gas but rather a liquid forced out of a can by a propellant. The aerosol (such as paint, stain, varnish, or hair spray) consists of tiny liquid droplets. The propellant gas that forces the liquid out of the can, such as butane, may be flammable. Aerosol sprays can be difficult to control, so care must be taken when spraying them near hot objects or open flames. Work in well-ventilated

Aerosol cans

Use a safety can to store and to transport gasoline, diesel fuel, and other flammable liquids.

areas to minimize your exposure and the buildup of flammable vapors. Additionally, the residue left behind from an aerosol spray can build up and create a flammable surface if ignited.

- **Flammable and combustible liquids** The most common sources of these materials include such fuels as gasoline, diesel fuel, kerosene, fuel oil/heating oil, and solvents, such as mineral spirits and paint thinner. Fuels are particularly dangerous due to their ability to be easily ignited and people's complacency when handling them for everyday uses, such as filling up a car or lawn mower with gasoline. Safe handling practices for flammable or combustible liquids include the following guidelines:
  - Use of proper containers. Keep fuel products, such as gasoline, diesel fuel, or kerosene, in steel containers called safety cans. These cans are engineered with a number of safety features specific to fuel products, including a metal design that allows for static electricity to be safely discharged, a self-closing spring-loaded pour spout, and an internal spark-arrest mechanism. Make sure that the can has a pressure-relief valve to allow ventilation of vapor.

■ Safe storage. Storing flammable products in the garage on the floor, away from ignition sources, is generally an adequate practice, because it is unlikely to cause a fire. However, it can contribute to the severity of a fire should one start, so a safer method of storage is a fire-rated metal cabinet. Fire-rated cabinets are designed to contain a fire inside of the cabinet should the materials stored there ignite, and these cabinets also prevent an outside fire from reaching the materials stored inside. Keep all flammable materials at least three feet away from ignition sources and review product labels and MSDSs for storage recommendations.

Where you do have combustion appliances, such as a furnace, be particularly mindful not to place flammable or combustible materials nearby or to cover the ventilation openings. Combustible materials can include paper, cardboard, or even rags.

■ Ignition source control. Prior to beginning any work involving flammable products, remove or extinguish all possible sources of ignition, such as hot metal parts; open flames, such as cigarettes or pilot lights (furnace, fire place, water heater); and static electric-

ity. Extinguish the ignition source, ventilate the work space to prevent the buildup of flammable vapors, or just work in another area free from ignition sources.

■ Careful usage practices. When transporting or using propane stored in a cylinder, keep the cylinder in the upright position. Never use combustion equipment (gasoline-powered motors, kerosene-powered heaters) indoors or in an enclosed garage. Confined engine exhaust can result in the buildup of poisonous carbon monoxide gas. Never use

Store flammable and combustible materials in an approved fire-rated cabinet for maximum protection.

flammable liquids as a cleaner, such as for paintbrushes or greasy engine parts.

- **Other notable fuel sources** Although each is not responsible for a large percentage of house fires, the following sources deserve mention:

  - Dryer lint. The accumulation of lint in or near the motor compartment of the dryer can result in a fire. Whether the dryer is powered by natural gas or electricity, lint buildup can combust when it comes into contact with a hot part of the motor. Refer to your dryer's operation manual for information on accessing and safely cleaning spaces where lint and dust can accumulate. In most cases, lint removal should be completed annually, but it depends on the amount of use the dryer gets.

  - Oily rags. The accumulation of oily/greasy rags in a pile or in a storage container can result in a fire. Oil and grease are organic materials, and the heat generated from their decay can result in spontaneous combustion. Exercise caution when storing oily rags for disposal or cleaning. It is best to let them dry out thoroughly before discarding them in an enclosed container, such as a garbage can.

  - Chimney fires. The accumulation of soot along the interior wall of a chimney can result in a fire. Chimney fires are mostly associated with wood or coal fireplaces. A spark from the fire can contact the soot built up in the chimney. Have your chimney cleaned at least one a year to minimize the potential of a fire, although the frequency of cleaning is dependent upon the frequency of use.

Fire Preparedness

Caution: Never fight a fire unless you have been trained. If a fire occurs, leave your home and dial 911.

Fire extinguishers work by suffocating the fire or by removing the ignition source. Extinguishers come in various sizes and contain an extinguishing agent designed for specific types of fires. If you own a fire extinguisher, you will need to make sure it is the correct type and size and is easily accessible. A fire extinguisher should not be kept close to areas that can catch fire. Access to it should be quick and safe. Good locations for keeping fire extinguishers handy include the kitchen and garage.

Fire extinguishers are rated according to the amount of extinguishing media they contain (typically five to ten pounds) and the type of fire they are designed to put out. Extinguishers are designed to fight fires of common materials grouped into classes A, B, C, D, and K, which include (respectively) paper or wood products, oil or petroleum products, electrical, metal, and vegetable oil/fat.

Inspect your extinguisher several times a year for the following:

- Make sure the extinguisher is not blocked by equipment, coats, or other objects that could interfere with accessing it in an emergency.
- Make sure the tank pressure is at the recommended level. On extinguishers equipped with a gauge, the needle should be in the green zone.
- Check to make sure the pin locking the handle is in place to prevent an unwanted discharge.
- Check for damage to the exterior, such as dents, leaks, rust, and chemical deposits.

If you believe your extinguisher is not in proper operating condition, have it inspected by a qualified

The fire extinguisher's label lists its rating.

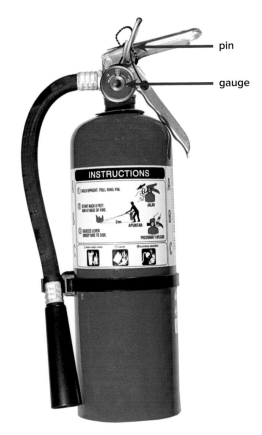

provider or purchase a new one. Finally, if you do need to use the extinguisher, remember the acronym **PASS** when fighting a fire: **P**ull the pin to release the handle; **A**im the extinguisher at the base of the fire; **S**queeze the trigger; **S**weep the discharge stream at the base of the fire. Empty the entire extinguisher, and don't turn your back on the fire. Only fight a fire at the incipient, or beginning, stages and when it is no larger than the size of a small trash can. Most home fire extinguishers do not contain the amount of extinguishing agent needed to battle a fire larger than this. Finally, if you end up using your extinguisher and it still has some extinguishing media left in it, do not reuse it. Once used, replace the extinguisher with a new one or have it recharged by a qualified service provider.

Smoke Detectors and Alarms

Smoke detectors and alarms save lives if they are maintained and used properly. If you don't have a working smoke detector in your home, *get one*. Smoke rises, so detectors are commonly installed on the ceiling. A separate detector needs to be placed on every level of your home, preferably just outside every bedroom, to ensure that wherever a fire starts, the smoke is detected immediately.

Smoke detectors are either wired directly into your home's electrical system or rely on batteries. Check your detectors periodically by pressing the "test" button. You should hear an audible alarm. If your detector alarm periodically "chirps," the battery is likely running low or the smoke sensor is failing. Don't ignore this sound. Determine the reason for the chirps and either service or

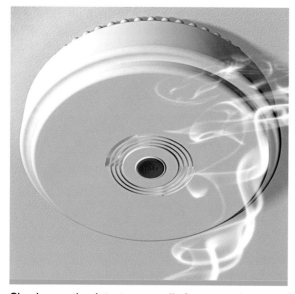

Check a smoke detector annually for proper functioning and replace batteries, if needed, twice a year.

replace the alarm. Test the detector twice a year (get into the habit of checking them when the time changes in the Fall and Spring) with a smoke source, such as the smoke from the end of a blown-out match. Do *not* disconnect the alarm if it goes off every time you cook. It is recommended to replace them at least every five years.

Finally, detectors only work if they can be heard. Test the alarm with your family members so they recognize the sound and know what to do if they hear it. Make sure the alarm can be heard with the bedroom doors

closed while everyone is asleep. Refer to Chapter 11, "Emergency Planning," for home fire drills and evacuation recommendations.

Recommended Practices

☑ Work in a well-ventilated area, preferably outside, to prevent the buildup of vapors. If necessary, use a fan to blow vapors outdoors.

☑ Eliminate all ignition sources, including hot objects and open flames, or shield or remove flammable material from the workspace.

☑ Clean up aerosol overspray and spills to eliminate flammable residues left behind. These areas can include the bathroom (hairspray) or garage (auto-maintainance or con-

struction products). Read the MSDS information for the product for recommendations on how to properly clean up a spill.

☑ Whenever your work could result in fire, keep a fire extinguisher handy.

☑ Never dispose of pressure cans or cylinders in a fire. Contact your city or county government environmental department for advice on proper disposal.

Proactive Safety

The following checklist can be used to help prevent and prepare for a fire in the home.

Fire Prevention and Preparedness Checklist

ITEM	CONDITION		ACTION		DATE
	OK ✔	NOT OK ✘	REPAIR ✔	REPLACE ✘	
Fire preparedness					
Are fire extinguishers located where they should be, and are they charged? Inspect them twice per year.					
Check your smoke alarms and batteries twice a year—commonly performed when daylight saving time begins and ends.					
Storage					
Are all liquids, gases, and aerosols stored in safe containers or cabinets? Inspect them monthly for leaks, spills, and container condition.					
Ignition Source					
Review the manufacturers' recommended schedules for checking igniters or ignition sources on your stove, furnace, water heater, and so forth.					
Keep all combustible material away from ignition sources by shielding or moving the material. Materials can include lint contained in dryer motor compartments, oily rags, paper products piled around combustion furnaces, or water heaters.					

RESOURCES

 The National Fire Protection Association (NFPA) has a vast amount of information regarding home fire safety, including stuff for kids, at http://www.nfpa.org.

 For additional information on propane safety, visit the Propane Education and Research Council at http://www.propane council.org.

 Underwriters Laboratory (UL) provides safety information, including electrical and fire prevention, at http://www.safetyathome.com.

For additional information on safe handling practices of flammable liquids and proper storage go to http://www.justritemfg.com.

I post current home-safety articles and information on my website at http://www.danshome safety.com.

Hand and Power Tools

Keizer 3-year-old saves dad by calling 911

"Hurry, my daddy needs help," said A.J., and then the phone was disconnected. The 9-1-1 operator attempted to call back while the dispatcher sent a Keizer Police officer to the location. A.J.'s father, Aaron Hayes, was leaning over the kitchen counter, bleeding profusely from his arm, when officer Scott Bigler arrived. He had impaled himself with a power tool and severed an artery. "I could have passed out and died in my own pool of blood, it was gushing that bad."

— KGWNews, Portland, OR, 28 January 2011

Hand and power tools make quick work of projects. As much as manufacturers claim their tools will last forever, we know better. Hammers and wrenches break, and power tools wear out. We often contribute to their failure by not using them as intended. This poor safety behavior often leads to accidents.

The common hazards associated with hand and power tool use include:

- **Pinch points** Hands are the part of the body that most often interact with the work at the point of contact, and they are therefore particularly susceptible to injury. Pinch points are created when the motion of your hand comes into contact with the nonmovable portion of the object you are working on. A pinch-point example might be your finger getting caught between the turning of a wrench and a lawn-mower blade or the space between the tool rest and the inward rotation of a sharpening wheel.

- **Electrocution** A metal wrench in your hand is a great conductor of electricity, which means you can get an electrical shock if while using it you come into contact with an exposed wire. If your power tool is operated electrically, you must take care to prevent electrical shock.
- **Cuts** A knife or rotating blade in a circular saw or chain saw can lead

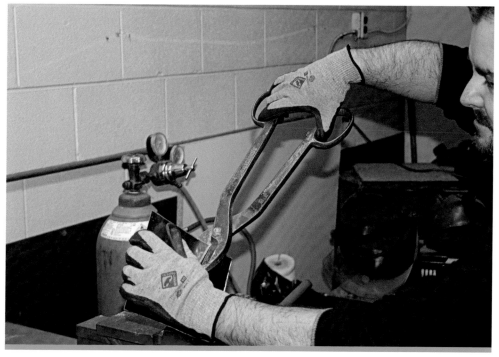

Cuts and pinched skin are the most common form of hand hazard in the home.

Flying objects are commonly present when you work with high-speed rotating power tools.

Use hand tools only for their intended purposes and keep them in top working condition to prevent injury.

to cuts, the loss of a finger, or even the loss of a hand.

- **Flying objects** Hand- or power-tool use can result in wood, metal, dirt, or other objects being thrown from the work area into the face and body.

Hand-Tool Safety

Hand tools require the forces of your body to complete the work, and we therefore risk injury to our muscles and joints. (Hand, arm, shoulder, and other associated injuries are discussed in greater detail in Chapter 10, "The Weekend Warrior.") The most important rule about using hand tools is to use them properly and only for their intended purposes. For instance, do not use a screwdriver as a chisel or a wrench as a hammer. If you have to modify the hand tool to get the job done, such as using a "cheater pipe" on the end of a wrench to increase your leverage, you really need a bigger wrench. Tools that are abused will fail, which then increases the likelihood of an injury. Keep tools in optimal working condition. A dull utility knife is much more danger-ous than a sharp knife, because you have to work harder with a dull knife to achieve the same results. Working in this way requires you to be more aggressive with the cutting action, which leads to injuries. Keep knife blades, chisel heads, saws, and even kitchen utensils sharp. Inspect your tools prior to use to identify cracks, excessive wear, or loose pieces. For striking surfaces, such as the head of a hammer or top of a chisel, watch for "mushrooming," which occurs when the striking surface flattens out and the metal edges that form can fly off when struck.

Power-Tool Safety

Power tools allow you to complete work in a fraction of the time. For the purpose of this discussion, power tools include hand- as well as push- or self-propelled engine- or motor-driven equipment (such as lawn mowers). Power tools can be powered by electricity, air (pneumatic), or gasoline/diesel.

Although cordless drills made by two different manufacturers complete the same task, safety features can vary from one to the next. *Read the owner's manual!* Even the seasoned power-tool user will benefit from reading the manufacturer's instructions, which contain safety-related precautions and warnings regarding proper use and maintenance.

Never deactivate or modify safety features. For instance, modern chain saws and lawn mowers are manufactured with interlocking mechanisms

missing guards

The flying object guard has been removed from this grinding wheel. Do not tamper with or remove safety features.

Allow the tool to do the work. Never force a tool!

that require you to depress a lever to allow the chain or blade to turn. Do not hold these switches down with tape to override this safety feature. Guards are a form of engineering control to prevent objects from flying into your face or keeping fingers out of places they shouldn't be. Do not remove or alter guards. If the work cannot be performed without removing the guard, either get a different tool to complete the work or read the owner's manual to see if the work can be performed safely with the guard removed.

Never force the tool to do something it can't. The idea is for the tool to do the hard work; by forcing it to perform in another capacity, you prevent the safety features from working properly. For electrical safety related to power tools, refer to Chapter 5, "Electrical Safety." Make sure any power tool you use is protected by a ground fault circuit interrupter (GFCI; for more information see page 50) and is equipped with a three-prong plug or is double insulated (refer to the owner's manual). A power tool that is double insulated protects the user from stray voltage and a short circuit by insulating the tool from the source of the short or the build-up of a stray electrical charge.

Finally, if you lose power or need to perform maintenance on the tool, turn the power tool switch to the "off" position to prevent unwanted startup when the power returns. Unplug the tool before performing maintenance and never run combustion equipment inside the home or garage, as this can result in the buildup of poisonous carbon monoxide gas.

Know Before You Buy

Prior to buying new tools or equipment, do your homework. Go to an equipment supply store and check the Internet or other reputable source to determine reliability and safety record for each make and model of tool.

Many injuries occur each year from homeowners trying to remove debris from rotating parts, such as in a snow blower, without turning the tool off first. Unplug or turn off your machine prior to performing maintenance. (© The Toro Company. All rights reserved.)

When purchasing tools, check the safety features. Pictured is SawStop's retracting blade mechanism that prevents the loss of fingers.

New products hit the market all the time. One such product that uses advanced engineering controls to make it considerably safer is the table saw illustrated on page 89. This saw uses an electrical sensor to stop the rotating blade in a fraction of a second when your skin accidentally touches it, allowing the blade to only nick your finger. When buying a tool, match your needs with the capabilities of the equipment. Purchasing a tool that is underpowered, too small, or meant for light-duty work when your work is heavy duty is sure to lead to an injury.

When Renting or Borrowing

When you're in a pinch and need a hand or power tool that you don't own, the options include purchasing a new one or, more likely, borrowing that tool from a neighbor or renting the needed tool. Take extra care when choosing either of these options, because you never know how well someone else's equipment has been cared for. As when you purchase a used car, you really don't know the condition of what you're getting. When renting a tool, make sure you take the time to have the rental staff instruct you on proper use and safety features. When using a rented piece, keep a close eye on the tool's performance. If pieces don't fit or fall off, don't "make it work" and continue to use it; call the rental place for a replacement. When borrowing a tool from a neighbor, take the same precautions as when you rent. Finally, remember that if you lend a tool, especially a power tool, to a neighbor and they injure themselves, they could sue you. So before you lend a tool, be certain that the borrower knows how to properly use it and that the borrower is safety conscious. Remember, safety is about managing your risks.

Recommended Practices

☑ Inspect hand and power tools prior to use. Read the owner's manual for information that describes normal versus excessive wear and other warning signs of improper function.

☑ Use a hand or power tool only for its intended purpose.

☑ Never modify the tool or bypass safety features, such as interlocking switches or guards.

☑ Perform scheduled maintenance. Keep your power tool in optimal and safe working condition. Refer to the owner's manual for maintenance schedules.

☑ Understand how your tool is powered and its associated hazards.

- Observe safe electrical practices when working with electric or battery-operated power tools. When working around electricity with hand tools (such as screwdrivers or wrenches), consider purchasing insulated tools. They are more expensive but add an extra layer of protection against electric shock.
- Remember that you're working with a flammable liquid when you operate fuel-powered tools. *Never* operate these tools indoors without proper ventilation.

- *Never* operate an air-powered (pneumatic) tool at an air pressure above the manufacturer's recommendation. An air compressor can be operated indoors only if it is powered electrically, as a fuel-powered compressor may cause buildup of poisonous carbon monoxide gas. Inspect fittings and air lines prior to each use for damage, and make sure they are compatible and rated for the same operating pressure. Release or bleed all compressed air at the completion of the project, including the compressor tank and air lines. Never leave anything under pressure.

☑ Observe all personal protective equipment (PPE) recommendations provided by the manufacturer. See Chapter 9, "Personal Protective Equipment," for additional recommendations on PPE use. In general, when operating hand and power tools, wearing safety glasses, work gloves, and hearing protection is recommended.

RESOURCES

 The Power Tool Institute (PTI) provides information on power-tool safety including free on-line videos, teaching instructions, and printable fact sheets for specific types of tools, at http://www.powertool institute.com/who.html.

 SawStop provides an innovative table saw breaking system to prevent injury. Information can be found at http://www.sawstop.com.

 Stihl provides power-tool-safety information including on-line videos at http://stihldealer.net /videolibrary.

Stanley Black and Decker provides information on safety and the proper use of hand and power tools at http://www.stanleyblackand decker.com.

Toro provides safety information for a variety of lawn and garden power tools at http://www.toro .com/en-us/safety/Pages/default.aspx.

I post current home-safety articles and information on my website at http://www.danshome safety.com.

Personal Protective Equipment

Roger, a veteran electrical construction worker, was completing a home renovation project when he received a wood sliver in his thumb. Although he was wearing cut-resistant gloves, they afforded little protection from punctures. A better choice would have been a leather glove. He tried removing the sliver with a pocket knife but could not and went about his business, having lived with dozens of slivers in his hand. After a day or so, his thumb swelled tremendously. Upon arriving at the emergency room, he was rushed to surgery to treat the aggressive staph infection (similar to flesh-eating bacteria) that was moving into his hand and arm. After surgery and aggressive antibiotic treatment, he found himself off work for more than three months. Roger continues to perform occupational therapy with hopes of returning to work soon.

— March 2011, Minneapolis, MN

Let's face it; wearing personal protective equipment (PPE) is cumbersome, uncomfortable, and unfashionable. PPE is equipment or clothing that is intended to cover or shield a part of your body to protect you against hazards. PPE commonly includes safety glasses, earplugs, a respirator, gloves, steel-toed boots, and outer protective clothing. PPE provides a "last line of defense" against bodily contact with a hazard, and it is personal—you select

it, you maintain it, and you choose to wear it (or not). Ask someone who has lost an eye whether they made the best choice about not wearing safety glasses.

PPE should not be your first consideration for protection from a hazard. Before you put on any PPE, you should determine whether the hazard can be eliminated through engineering or administrative controls, as discussed in Chapter 3, "Safety Basics." For your PPE to work effectively, you must religiously observe the following guidelines:

- Wear it every time, without fail, and wear it according to the manufacturer's recommendations.
- Maintain it to ensure proper working condition. Clean it and inspect it prior to each use for excessive wear and tear. Take care of it, and it will take care of you.

PPE must be matched to the hazard. Improper selection of this glove has likely resulted in acid burns to the hand, as evidenced by the holes.

- Make sure it is the right type for the hazards present. For example, the photo at the left shows what happens when the wrong glove is selected for use with a cleaning chemical containing an acid. Acid easily "eats" through the cotton glove, resulting in minor burns to the back of the hand.

When purchasing PPE, look for items that have been manufactured to standards established by the American National Standards Institute (ANSI) or American Society of Testing and Materials (ASTM). These standards establish performance tolerances under specific occupational conditions. Make sure respirators have been approved by the National Institute of Occupational Safety and Health (NIOSH). Cheap PPE is usually not the best PPE. Read the manufacturer's instructions on how to properly wear, inspect, and maintain your PPE. Consider the various types of PPE and what parts of the body they protect.

Protect Your Head and Face

- **Head** It is unlikely that a homeowner will have an occasion to wear a hard hat, so this book does

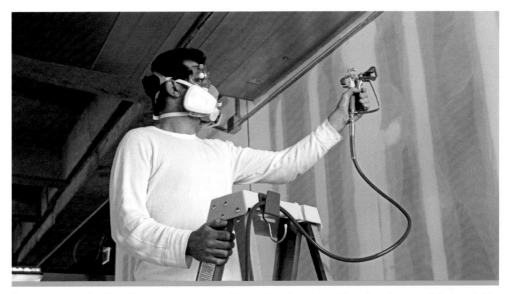

Purchase PPE that has been approved by **ANSI, ASTM,** or **NIOSH** and make sure it is the right type for the job.

not address them. However, there are certainly occasions and situations in and around the home when the use of a hard hat is advisable.

- **Eyes** Protect your eyes at all costs! They are precious and irreplaceable. Protective eyewear is recommended for most activities where flying wood, metal, or other objects may be present. Select safety glasses that have an ANSI Z87.1 rating, which indicates they offer a sufficient level of protection for home or workplace use (this rating is usually indicated on the packaging or on the ear piece). Choose glasses that wrap around the side of the eye to provide full protec-

tion. Many styles of safety glasses are available, including ones with darkened or tinted glasses for outside activities.

Protect your eyes with safety glasses or goggles as necessary.

A face shield, respirator, and earmuffs being used by a safety-conscious person

If you need to wear prescription glasses when you work, you have a couple of options: Select safety glasses that are extra large and fit over your prescription glasses or purchase prescription safety glasses. If you frequently

Silicone earplugs

handle hazardous liquids, wear safety goggles that provide a liquid-tight seal around the eye socket.

- **Face** Full face protection is achieved with the use of a face shield. A face shield can be constructed of clear plastic or metal mesh, depending upon the hazards present. A banding strap attaches to the shield to hold it in place on the head. Face shields are recommended where larger or more frequent flying objects, such as wood chips or metal pieces, are expected to come into contact with the face.

- **Ears** Once your hearing is lost, you can't get it back. Even short, repeated exposure to moderately high levels of noise can cause hearing loss over time. Consider a home project in which you use a circular saw to cut lumber for a deck. Just the few seconds it takes to cut the lumber negatively affects the unprotected ear. Multiply that impact by one hundred or two hundred over the life of the project, and the damage adds up. The two most commonly used forms of hearing protection are earplugs and earmuffs. Both are suitable for most home applications. Common foam or silcone earplugs are inserted into the ear canal, and they are lightweight and disposable. They must be inserted properly into the ear to achieve maximum protection. Earmuffs are heavier and protect by covering the entire outer ear. Anything other than an engineered earplug should not be used. This includes cotton balls, cloth, or ear buds from music headphones.

The rule of thumb with noise is that if you must raise your voice above a normal conversation level at a distance of three feet from the person you are talking to, you need to wear hearing protection. Most newly manufactured power tools list the noise output in the owner's manual. If that noise level is greater than eighty-five decibels (dB), you definitely need to wear hearing protection.

- **Respiratory** The quality of the air you breathe can have both short- and long-term effects on your health. Dusts, mists, fumes, aerosols, and gases can be dangerous when inhaled. Building materials that pose potential hazards include paint dust (lead), sheetrock dust (silica), floor tile (asbestos), solvents, pesticides, welding fumes, and fiberglass insulation. Inhalation is the quickest route of exposure due to the rapid absorption into the body through the blood stream. Inhalation is of greatest concern in enclosed (confined) spaces where ventilation is difficult, such as bathroom shower stalls, crawl spaces, or attics.

A properly selected and worn respirator protects the body from inhalation hazards. To keep your inhalation exposure to a minimum, observe the following guidelines:

- Work outside. If you must work inside, ventilate the room to the outside using fans. Avoid working in a small room with no open

A paper face mask provides good protection against inhaling dust.

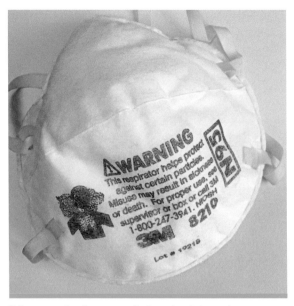

When purchasing a respirator, check to make sure you are selecting the right one for the job. Is your hazard dust, welding fumes, paint, or solvents?

A typical respirator is designed to cover the nose and mouth to filter the air you breathe. It is held in place with straps that go around the back of the head. Most white-paper masks found in home-supply stores are used to protect against dust. For protection from dust, look for a mask marked with the term "HEPA," which stands for high efficiency particulate air filter. These are designed to trap 99.97 percent of all particles 0.3 microns in size (much smaller than the diameter of your hair) or larger. Paper masks are fairly inexpensive and disposable.

Respirators that are made of rubber or silicone are designed to be reused but require filter cartridges. You must select the right type of filter cartridge for the hazard. Read the packaging or ask for assistance from store staff. Remember, you must have the right type of respirator to provide adequate protection!

Proper fit of a respirator is just as important as selection. Not all faces are the same shape and size, which means the first respirator you purchase may not work for you; you may have to purchase another style or brand to achieve a tight seal and proper fit. In the working world, professionals wearing respirators must be fit-tested to ensure a proper seal around the face and optimal respira-

doors or windows. A lack of ventilation can be especially dangerous if you are using a flammable product.

- Use a nontoxic product. Some materials are listed as no or low "VOCs," which refers to a low concentration of volatile organic compounds that are commonly found in paints, stains, and solvents.
- Read the product label and heed the precautions. Abide by the manufacturer's recommendations for the products you're using and know the warning signs of overexposure, such as a headache, nausea, and blurred vision.

tor performance. To achieve proper fit of your respirator, read the manufacturer's instructions. Additionally, take the following precautions:

- Men must be clean shaven to ensure a tight seal around the face.
- Do not modify the respirator by cutting holes in it or changing its size or shape.
- If you are wearing a cartridge respirator that is fitted properly and working properly, you should not smell any chemical odors inside the mask. If you do smell odors inside the mask, one of two things is occurring: The mask does not fit properly or the filtering cartridge is spent and is no longer filtering the air. If either of these things is the case, you need move out of the work area to determine the reason for the respirator's not working properly.
- The respirator should not be pressed against the face so tightly that you get a headache.
- Clean and maintain the respirator properly. Take care of it, and it will take care of you.

Protect Your Hands

Your hands are more likely to contact a hazard than any other part of your body. Gloves provide a protective barrier between you and a cut, burn, scratch, sliver, dermatitis (dry flaking skin), or even the loss of a finger. Gloves can be constructed of cotton, leather, nitrile, neoprene, latex, and Kevlar. One size and type does *not* fit all, so as with a respirator, the key is to select the pair that is appropriate to protect against the hazard.

A common complaint from people who wear gloves is the loss of dexterity or feeling between the work and their fingers. Work gloves have

Select and use gloves to protect against the specific hazard.

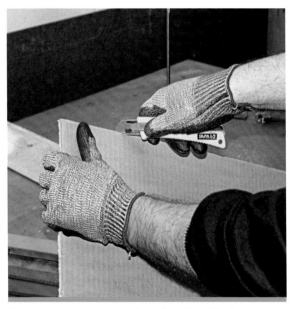

Cut-resistant gloves are durable without losing any dexterity or sense of feeling with the work.

a greater hazard, such as when you're feeding lumber through a table saw. If for some reason the board should pull into the blade and your glove catches on the wood, it could pull your hand into the saw.

Whether you're cleaning your toilet, staining wood, or using a chain saw, you should wear gloves to protect your hands from chemical or physical hazards. The performance of a pair of gloves is determined by the manufacturer, who tests the gloves' ability to withstand a variety of chemicals. As when you select any other piece of PPE, identify the hazard (chemical ingredients on the product label) and then read the PPE packaging to make sure it will provide adequate protection from the hazard. Table 9.1 below lists the recommended types of gloves for common chemical and physical hazards.

evolved over the last several years and are more protective, tighter fitting, and thinner, which allows for a better sense of "feeling" with the work. It should be noted that in some instances, wearing gloves could present

TABLE 9.1. Glove Selection Recommendations

Hazard	Recommended Glove
Acids and bases (drain cleaner, pool cleaners, and disinfectants)	Nitrile or neoprene
Cutting, sawing, sharp tool use	Leather or Kevlar
Fuels (gasoline, diesel, kerosene)	Nitrile
Paint	Nitrile
Pesticides and fertilizers	Nitrile
Petroleum solvents (mineral spirits)	Nitrile

Protect Your Feet

Although homes typically do not present a lot of crushing hazards, there are occasions where sturdy work boots equipped with steel toes would be of value, such as when as moving heavy objects (landscape rocks, heavy furniture, etc.). Steel-toed footwear has come a long way and is much more stylish than the stereotypical heavy boot. It can even be found in the form of a tennis shoe. A steel-toe component comes in handy where there is a threat from heavy objects dropping on your foot or your being cut, but even if a steel toe is not completely necessary around the house, wearing a boot that covers the ankle will add support and help prevent ankle sprains.

For the best protection against dry or liquid chemicals contacting your feet, purchase a pair of rubber boots, which can be easily cleaned with a scrub brush and a garden hose.

Rubber boots provide excellent protection against many dry and liquid chemicals. They do not absorb chemicals and can be easily cleaned.

Protect the Rest of Your Body

On most occasions, denim pants and a short- or long-sleeved T-shirt provide adequate body protection, but take a few minutes to evaluate the project and determine what parts of the body may come into contact with potential hazards.

If you are completing a messy project, you may not want to get your clothes excessively dirty and con-taminate your home washing machine with the material. Such is the case with sheet-rock dust, paint, or stain. For tasks that will create or require these materials, consider wearing a lightweight disposable coverall, such as a Tyvec suit manufactured by DuPont. These inexpensive coveralls are ideal for keeping dust and the occasional liquid splash off your

Tyvec suits provide good protection from dust, paint spray, and other nonpenetrating chemicals.

clothing. A suit designed to protect you from dust will likely not work if the hazard is a chemical.

Cotton aprons, smocks, or coveralls also protect the body against contact with hazardous materials or tools. If you work with an open flame, weld, or are around items that can cause a thermal burn, consider wearing fire- or flame-resistant clothing, such as Nomex. This material is comparable to what firefighters wear but can be found in lightweight coveralls.

Recommended Practices

Table 9.2 lists the recommended types of PPE for various household activities.

TABLE 9.2. Recommended PPE Selection

Activity	Recommended PPE
Trimming and cutting the grass	Safety glasses or face shield, hearing protection, leather gloves, long pants, work boots
Power washing (car or house)	Safety glasses or face shield, hearing protection, long pants, leather gloves
Painting, staining, or cleaning (disinfectants, cleansers, and so forth)	Chemical-resistant gloves, long-sleeve shirt and pants, safety glasses, respirator if recommended by the manufacturer or working in enclosed spaces
Power tool use (such as circular or table saw)	Safety glasses or face shield, hearing protection, gloves
Vacuuming (shop-vac in enclosed areas)	Hearing protection
Sanding or other activity generating dust	Respirator (preferably one with a **HEPA** filter), safety glasses, hearing protection

RESOURCES

 For technical assistance in selecting a respirator, call the 3M Technical Assistance number (800) 243-4630. 3M offers additional information on all the lines of 3M PPE at its occupational health and environmental safety website, http://www.3M.com/OccSafety.

 Tilsatec manufactures a full line of protective glove apparel. For more glove-selection assistance visit http://www.tilsatec.com.

Stihl manufactures a full line of PPE for use with power tools. For more information visit http://www.stihl.com.

Dupont manufacturers Tyvec-brand coveralls and provides assistance in the selection of body coverings. For more information visit http://www2.dupont.com/Tyvek/en_US/index.html.

I post current home-safety articles and information on my website at http://www.danshomesafety.com.

CHAPTER 10

The Weekend Warrior

Homeowner suffers crippling back spasm while landscaping—ruins weekend

While working on day two of his project laying a paver side-walk in front of his house, Mr. Dan Hannan of Roberts, WI, said he felt something "pop" in his back. "My back was a little sore and tight from the day before, but I thought I could gut it out to finish the project. After it popped, I literally crawled into the house. Maybe I should have eased into the day, warmed up a bit, or just taken the day off. Maybe I was dehydrated, too. It sure is tough getting old."

— RealFakeArticles.com, May 2000

You wake up early on a Saturday, excited to get that landscape project started. You get dressed, eat some breakfast, and head to the garage to begin building a retaining wall. You bend down and start moving those landscape blocks and then it happens—you pull a back muscle. The project is over before it gets started.

In the world of construction, soft-tissue injuries, such as sprains and strains, account for many disabling injuries. To combat this problem, many contractors are now implementing stretching programs that require workers to warm up at the start of each day. Imagine a workforce of five hundred carpenters, electricians, cement masons, and plumbers all doing back bends at 6:00 AM at the building site of a new baseball stadium. This scenario occurs more frequently than you think, because stretching programs help prevent serious injury.

Just as important as warming up and easing into your work is the way in which you use your body. Your body mechanics and body positioning when lifting determine the strain on your back and hamstring muscles. The goal is to use your body in the most efficient way possible while keeping stress and strain to a minimum. Repeated abuse of your body can result in chronic joint and muscle problems. Remember, your back is not a crane, and you shouldn't let your stubbornness override common sense in quitting when your body has had enough. Fatigue leads to loss of concentration and body control, which often means an accident is close behind.

If you're not a construction worker or otherwise physically active, the first thing to admit is that your enthusiasm to complete a project is likely going to result in spending the next day or two nursing a sore body. It can be difficult sometimes to gauge the

Construction workers stretching to start the day (Courtesy of Brandon Dill, Special to the Commercial Appeal)

damage you inflict upon your body, such as not realizing how badly you are becoming sunburned until the next day. Don't overdo it. Go slowly, and set reasonable project goals.

Even a simple task that involves working overhead with your arms can lead to significant muscle strain if you are not conditioned to it.

As with all work activity, allow your body to warm up and don't push yourself to the point of exhaustion.

Complete a heavy-duty task by taking frequent breaks or working on it over several days. A little planning, combined with a reality check, goes a long way toward preventing injury. Consider the following guidelines to help keep your overzealous intentions in check:

- **Degree of difficulty** Is the project light duty (raking leaves), medium duty (shoveling sand), or heavy duty (moving landscape blocks)? Ask for help or utilize power equipment.
- **Length of the project** Don't try to beat the setting sun to complete the project in one day if it is really a two-day job.
- **Environmental conditions** Are you working in high heat and humidity? Doing so places a tremendous burden on the body. Heat-related stress can be very dangerous and result in heat exhaustion or heatstroke. Take frequent breaks and drink fluids that include electrolytes (such as Gatorade).
- **Equipment** Where possible, utilize power material-handling equipment to lighten wear and tear on your body. There is a reason why you have the ability to rent a trenching machine from the equipment-rental store down the street. If rental is not for you, consider contracting with a professional.
- **Health** In northern climates, certain snowfalls are called "heart-attack snows." Unfit individuals who are shoveling wet, heavy snow often results in a medical emergency. Participate in an exercise program to maintain muscle strength and cardiovascular fitness. Don't overdo it—pace yourself!

Warm-Up Stretches

Injury prevention starts with warming up the body. Regardless of your age or gender, your muscles need to warm up and have good blood flow. When working, you lift, pull, push, carry, and reach, which places strain on muscles, ligaments, and tendons. Several simple stretches should be completed before the start of a day's worth of household chores and projects. When performing any stretch or activity, start out slowly and easily, and if it hurts, stop! The following four stretches will help you warm up major muscle groups.

Lower-back bend. With your feet set a shoulders' width apart, place a hand behind each hip bone and support your lower back with your fingers. Slowly arch your back and hold the position for three to five seconds. Repeat two or three times.

Side bend. With your feet set a shoulders' width apart, raise one hand over your head and slowly reach to the opposite side. Keep both feet flat on the ground and hold the stretch for three to five seconds. Repeat twice on both sides.

Hamstring stretch. Choose a sturdy, stable object—like a tread on a flight of stairs—that is at least ten inches in height. Place one foot on the object and slowly bend forward at the hip. Hold at a comfortable position for five to ten seconds. Switch legs and repeat twice for each leg.

Chest and shoulder stretch. While standing straight, raise your arms with elbows bent and your upper arms parallel to the ground. Slowly squeeze your shoulder blades together, pushing your chest out. Hold for three to five seconds and repeat three times.

Body Positioning and Lifting

People often associate muscle injury or strain with pushing their bodies to, or beyond, the limit. However, something as simple as reaching for a sock on the floor can result in your back "going out" or cause a spasm. Good body mechanics, or the way you use your body, can prevent an injury today and chronic problems years down the road. Ask yourself the following questions before you undertake any lifting, pushing, pulling, or carrying activity:

- Is my body in the best position to keep the strain to a minimum?
- Is there a tool or piece of equipment that I can use instead of my body?
- Can I get someone to help me?

Improper lifting. *Never* bend at the waist to pick up any object. The forces placed on your lower back are tremendous in this position. *Never* lift and twist at the waist to set down or to pick up an object.

Proper lifting. Kneel on one leg to position your body close to the object or pull the object toward you. Keep the object as close to your body as possible. With your back straight and your head forward, slowly stand. If the object is too heavy or large, apply the same technique, combining the efforts of two people.

Lifting properly while placing minimal strain on the back requires the use of three key muscle groups—the hips, thighs, and stomach. If you exercise, work on strengthening these muscle groups. Consider the techniques illustrated at the bottom of the previous page when lifting an object.

Material-Handling Equipment

What do you think is easier, moving a wheelbarrow full of dirt or a dozen five-gallon buckets full of dirt? Shovels, two-wheel dollies, wheelbarrows, pulleys, and other common tools all employ the basic principles of physics to make jobs easier. How about mechanical leverage? That's demonstrated through the use of a long-handled shovel to pry a rock out of the ground. Next time, try to complete the task with a shovel whose handle is half the length. You have to work a lot harder to get the same result.

The objective is to use a powered or manually operated piece of equipment to lessen the strain on your body. Whenever possible, employ a mechanical device to help you lift,

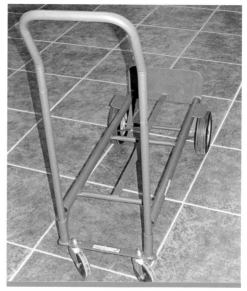

This dolly is convertible from its upright function and can be used as a four-wheel pushcart.

pull, push, or roll an object from one place to another. Make sure you check the capacity or safe limits of the rope, pulley, or equipment you are using. Never use equipment or material that is not designed to accommodate the load and strain you are placing on it. Don't be a scrooge and opt for swinging a sledgehammer when the rental place down the block rents electric jackhammers by the half day. Your body will thank you tomorrow.

Table 10.1 lists some of the more common household material-handling devices to consider pur-

Straps and lifting aids, such as these straps that fit over the forearms, provide assistance with lifting.

chasing and also describes what they are used for.

TABLE 10.1. Material-Handling Equipment and Its Uses

Item	Uses
Wheelbarrows	Moving large quantities of loose material, such as rock, sand, gravel, wood chips, or anything else that fits inside.
Two-wheel dollies	Moving appliances or anything else that can be positioned to fit on its front fork. Certain dollies are equipped with different configurations for pulling horizontally or for moving large items up and down stairs.
Pulleys	Lifting or hoisting objects. Uses include suspending objects from the ceiling of a garage or workspace. Never place anything that you don't want damaged, including youself, under a suspended load.
Forearm lifting straps	Moving large, bulky items, such as furniture and mattresses.
Pushcarts	Moving large, heavy items horizontally.

CHAPTER 11
Emergency Planning

Students, residents feel tornado's effects

"When [the tornado] hit, the house lifted up off of us, and then a Jeep Cherokee came right over us and hit me in the head. We were underneath the Jeep on our knees and chest for the end of it. After we got hit, we pulled five or six people out, but it was gone. The house was gone."

— Adam Melton, 28 April 2011, the *Crimson White*

No one likes emergencies, especially those that threaten their families. Unless you are a firefighter, police officer, or some other emergency-services professional, you likely will not respond well in an emergency situation unless you are prepared. How well you react to an emergency depends on your level of confidence and familiarity with the situation. Even the scariest occurrences can become manageable if you experience them often enough. For instance, the first time a loved one has an epileptic seizure can be a terrifying experience, but by the tenth time you are able to manage the situation more calmly and properly.

Following the total engine failure of a fully loaded commercial airplane on 19 January 2009, the pilot, Captain Chesley "Sully" Sullenberger, successfully landed the aircraft on the Hudson River in New York, with no lives lost. Do you think that was the first time he ever encountered that situation? It wasn't, because pilots continuously practice on flight simulators to

Thank you, Captain Sullenberger! (Photo courtesy of the Associated Press.)

increase their situational awareness during emergencies. This familiarity lets them perform correctly when it counts. However, even highly trained and experienced individuals can still panic in emergency situations. The only thing you can do is control what you can by taking reasonable steps to prepare yourself to succeed rather than fail in an emergency.

Absent the desire or ability to experience something terrible over and over to develop a calm response, you can choose to better prepare yourself by planning and practicing for emergencies. You can't anticipate every type of home emergency, but you can prepare for the most probable causes, which include medical crises, severe weather, and fires.

First Aid and CPR

If you have not completed a first-aid and CPR course within the last two years, you need to. Like any other skill you acquire, if you don't use it, you lose it. Knowing first aid and CPR will arm you with basic life-saving skills, such as how to help someone who is choking or having a heart attack or how to give first-aid for cuts, objects in the eye, or even insect bites that may cause someone to go into shock. Refresh your memory often, as first-aid/CPR techniques change and new devices enter the marketplace. For instance, the use of automatic external defibrillation (AED) devices is commonplace in large venues and is even making its way into homes. Knowing how to use this type of a device increases your chances of sav-

ing a heart-attack victim. If you have infants, make sure your CPR class addresses reviving infants, as the techniques used for assisting them differ from those for an adult. Don't be afraid to lend a hand, even if your knowledge is rusty. In nearly all cases, the Good Samaritan law applies, allowing you to administer first aid and CPR assistance without the fear of being named in a lawsuit.

A familiar—and useful—symbol

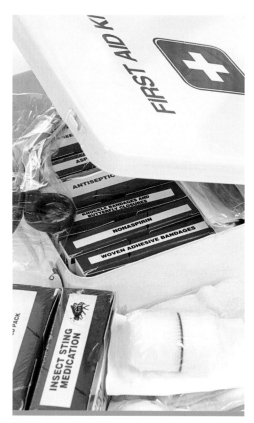

First-aid kits only work if they are adequately stocked and you know how to use the supplies.

Equip your home and automobiles with first-aid kits. Inspect the kits periodically to make sure everything is there and nothing has expired (such as ointments, salves, liquids, or sterile items). Make sure everyone in the home knows where the first-aid kits are located and how to summon emergency assistance via 911. For chemical-exposure and poisoning situations contact the Poison Center at (800) 222-1222.

Facing Severe Weather

Few places in the United States are exempt from experiencing some type of severe weather. Tornados, hurricanes, earthquakes, blizzards, floods, wildfires, mud slides, and other natural disasters result in millions of dollars in property damage and loss of life annually. Some of these occurrences are more sudden than others and require the following extra attention to preparedness:

- Be proactive and know your town, city, and county emergency-response capabilities and plans. Most municipalities and counties have designated staff to help coordinate local resources for assistance, including communicating with residents. These government officials are responsible for planning and carrying out emergency plans, such as evacuations. Contact your local emergency-preparedness official and get to know the agency's capabilities, plans, and what it expects from citizens in a time of crisis. Ask for literature and even a copy of any prepared emergency plans.
- Know your emergency alert system. What does it look like and sound like, and how does it communicate with you? Civil-defense

sirens, television programs, radio spots, e-mail or text notifications, telephone calls, and other means of communication all allow for the broadcasting of mass alerts. Ask yourself, "If I am asleep, how do I know if there is an emergency?" Living in rural areas is particularly challenging if you cannot hear a civil-defense siren. Consider purchasing a severe weather–alert radio that runs on electricity and battery backup in the event the power goes out. This programmable radio broadcasts severe weather alerts via loud automatic messages through the National Weather Service. This type of radio is portable, so it can be taken on trips as well.

Emergency-alert radios provide warnings of approaching severe weather at home and on the road.

- Establish a family-response plan and practice it at least twice a year. Most communities sponsor a severe-weather week to get residents in the mind-set of preparedness. Your plan should include actions that are easy to remember and implement, such as identifying common exit routes in the home or choosing areas outside the home in which to gather (muster locations). For instance, for tornado threats, identify the most structurally sound room in your home and let everyone know that this is the designated shelter. Don't forget the possibility of having to stay in that location for some time or even possibly being trapped. Plan ahead and keep a bin in that location with such supplies as nonperishable foods, flashlights, a radio, bottled water, a first-aid kit, and other items necessary for your family.

- *Pay attention!* Watch local weather reports or TV news. There is no excuse for not taking action when signs of severe weather develop.

Rope ladders can be used to escape a home in an emergency when other means of escape are blocked. (Photo courtesy Florence Supply Co.)

Dealing with Fires

Fires can start almost anywhere in a home and for a variety of reasons. More information regarding preventing and responding to fires is contained in Chapter 7, "Fire Prevention and Preparedness." Fire education, especially for children, is critical when it comes to responding to a fire emergency properly. The most important thing to tell children is to never try to extinguish the fire; instead, everyone should exit the home immediately. A properly prepared and practiced fire drill saves lives. Practice a drill at least every three or four months so the actions stay fresh in everyone's minds. When developing a fire-exit plan and drill, consider the following factors:

- Visualize every room in the house and think of your planned response to a fire starting in each. How would you respond if preferred exits were not accessible due to the fire? Would you need to go through a window?
- Think through a fire on each level if you live in a multilevel home. Consider using windows as exits. If you are two or more stories above the ground, consider leaving a rope ladder in each room that can be quickly anchored and

lowered outside the window for climbing to safety.

- Understand that smoke rises. Smoke from home fires is often toxic and can kill just as easily as the fire itself. Teach family members the concept of crawling along the floor where the air is better and feeling doorknobs or the doors for heat on the other side before opening them.
- Place a smoke detector on every level of the home if you have not already done so, and verify that each is working properly. Replace batteries, if required, at least annually. Smoke detectors save thousands of lives every year. Make sure everyone understands what the detector alarm sounds like and test it at night when everyone is sleeping with the doors closed to ensure everyone can hear it.

RESOURCES

The Federal Emergency Management Agency (FEMA) provides federal coordination of assistance following national disasters. Information regarding disaster preparation and relief can be found at http://www.fema.org.

The American Red Cross provides information regarding home preparedness for emergency events and training services for first aid and CPR. Information is available at http://www.redcross.org.

The National Fire Protection Association (NFPA) provides information regarding home fire safety, including stuff for kids, at http://www.nfpa.org.

The Federal Alliance for Safe Homes (FLASH) promotes disaster safety and property loss mitigation with on-line videos and free literature at http://www.flash.org.

I post current home-safety articles and information on my website at http://www.danshome safety.com.

CHAPTER 12

Indoor Air-Quality Exposures

Mold making Atlanta homeowners sick — Tough questions for Fair Walker Townhomes' developer, builder

Now Kesha McNair and several other homeowners who live and work in the Fair Walker Townhomes in downtown Atlanta have a problem with mold. "That's affecting my business, it's affecting the comfort of my home, and it's also starting to affect my health," said Anita Busbee. McNair hired a mold inspector to test her home. McNair said, "The first thing that man told me is 'Move, you need to move.'"

— Tony McNary, CBS Atlanta Reporter, WCGL television broadcast, 1 February 2010

Depending on the materials used in your home's construction and what other homeowners before you may have done, the air in your home may pose a real health threat from such substances as carbon monoxide, lead, mercury, mold, asbestos, and radon. With the exception of carbon monoxide, all the previously mentioned substances are usually related to chronic or long-term health problems. The primary routes of exposure are inhalation (breathing) and ingestion, usually through hand-to-mouth activities. Air quality inside and outside your home is important, but in some cases, exposure to the building materials through contact or simply breathing the indoor air can result in significant health problems. Buildings that pose these problems are said to be "sick," a condition otherwise known as "sick building syndrome."

To completely and accurately evaluate the health of your home and determine whether it presents any of the exposures referenced above, you should employ professional help from an indoor air-quality specialist or a certified industrial hygienist.

Danger: Carbon Monoxide

Carbon monoxide (CO—its chemical formula) is often referred to as the "silent killer," because it is odorless, colorless, and tasteless. CO is a by-product of combustion, with the most common source being a home's furnace not operating properly. CO gas is considered a chemical asphyxiant. It suffocates and kills because, once inhaled, it is two hundred times more efficient at attaching to red blood cells than oxygen, causing the body to lose its ability to move oxygen through the bloodstream. When concentrations of CO build up in the home, its effect on the body can include moderate to severe headaches, nausea, and narcosis, a state of sleepiness or loss of consciousness. If you are sleeping when CO builds up in the home, chances are you won't wake up. An early warning sign of possible CO poisoning would be if more than one person

Furnaces, even high-efficiency models, can run poorly, resulting in the release of CO gas.

develops a headache at nearly the same time. If this occurs, get out of the house immediately, dial 911, and allow the fire department to ventilate the home. CO is not a combustible or explosive gas, so don't worry about a home explosion. Do not reenter the home until you are told it is safe to do so. Contact a furnace specialist to inspect and to repair your furnace immediately.

Recommended Practices

- Have your furnace, fireplace, and any other combustion appliance in the home inspected annually by a qualified provider.
- *Never* run combustion equipment inside the home that is not intended for indoor use, such as portable generators or heaters that run on gasoline, diesel fuel, or kerosene.
- Never run your car in a closed garage, especially where the garage is attached to the house. Open the garage door before starting the engine.
- Place a carbon-monoxide detector on each level of your house and test them every month. Read the manufacturer's information and pay special attention to the anticipated lifespan of the detector. Detectors use chemical sensors to detect CO and thus wear out over time. Some detectors will alert you of the sensor failure, but others will not.
- Make sure your home pulls fresh air from outside for the heating, ventilation, and air-conditioning system (HVAC). Modern homes are constructed "tight," or well insulated, and require air-exchange systems to pull fresh outside air inside.

Danger: Lead

Lead is particularly harmful to children under the age of six. Lead in the bloodstream can cause neurological development problems. The primary source of lead exposure in homes is paint. Lead paint found on toys, especially those manufactured in China, has drawn considerable attention from the U.S. government over the last several years and is now heavily monitored. Lead-based wall paint was used extensively in homes for interior and exterior applications until 1978, when it was banned from use. Unless lead paint has been painted over with nonlead paint or removed, it can continue to pose an exposure hazard. Exposure occurs when your hand or clothing contacts the lead-paint surface, allowing the transfer of dust. From there, the dust enters the body through hand-to-mouth contact or by inhaling the dust. The exposure potential goes up significantly when you disturb the lead-paint surface by sanding, drilling, or cutting.

Proper lead abatement often requires engineering and PPE controls to ensure there is no exposure. (Photo courtesy of Inline Distribution Company)

Breathing lead dust is particularly hazardous during home repair or do-it-yourself projects. Multiple coats of nonlead-based paint may cover lead-based paint in older homes. As of April 2010, the U.S. Environmental Protection Agency (EPA) requires all commercial contractors completing repairs, renovations, or paint jobs for homeowners living in pre-1978 homes to determine whether lead paint is present. Determination can be completed by collecting a sample and sending it to a testing laboratory. If lead paint is present, the contractor performing the work is required to hold certification issued by the EPA verifying that they are qualified to perform work that disturbs lead-coated surfaces. Contractors are required to follow strict procedures to minimize a homeowner's exposure to lead dust. When work begins at your home, inside or outside, control of lead dust is achieved by building enclosures with the use of plastic sheeting. The sheeting will trap lead dust that is generated during sanding or cutting activities. The contractor is also obligated to provide you with pamphlet information about the hazards. All dust and wood chips must be either swept up or vacuumed and disposed of as hazardous waste.

Federal law does not require you to hire a certified contractor when lead paint is present—you can work on your home yourself. If you choose to work on your house where you suspect or know lead-based paint is present, adhere to the following EPA recommendations:

- Have paint samples tested for the presence of lead by contracting with a local assessment company.
- Consider hiring an EPA-certified contractor to handle repairs in areas where you know lead paint is present. A list of companies can be found through the EPA website. Check the contractor's certification credentials prior to starting the work and hire people who are properly bonded and insured. Check the contractor's references or obtain work references for jobs that have been performed for others, and contact the Better Business Bureau to see if any complaints have been registered against the company.
- Be mindful of your exposure levels if you choose to do the work yourself. Complete a hazard analysis as discussed in Chapter 3, "Safety Basics." You should at a minimum observe the following guidelines:
  - Isolate areas where you may generate dust from those that are clean by closing interior doors and windows or, for smaller areas, cordoning off the workspace with plastic sheeting draped from floor to ceiling.
  - Remove all furniture and other movable items from the room.

- Collect dust using vacuums with high efficiency particulate air (HEPA) filters. Place the dust into a sealable container and deliver it to your local household hazardous waste collection facility.
- Wipe all surfaces with disposable paper or cloth towels and water to remove the remaining dust. Do this at least twice. Discard towels into the trash.
- At the very least, wear the following PPE items:
  - HEPA half-face respirator, or HEPA dust mask. This will provide good protection for dust forms of lead. However, if you are heating lead paint for removal, your respirator may not provide adequate protection from the smoke or fumes. Please refer to the respirator manufacturer's recommendations for use limitations and care.
  - goggles (rather than safety glasses)
  - disposable gloves, such as nitrile or latex gloves
  - a disposable body suit, such as one made of Tyvec, rather than bringing your dusty lead-covered clothes into your washer and dryer areas
- Clean up immediately afterward by thoroughly showering.

Danger: Mercury

Mercury is another central nervous system disrupter. Mercury is commonly found in the home as a liquid or powder and can be absorbed through the skin or inhaled as a vapor that is colorless, odorless, and tasteless. Although some older adults may remember playing with liquid mercury as children, it is toxic. Household sources include older dial-style thermostat controls, thermometers, and compact fluorescent lights (CFLs).

Thermostats and Thermometers

If you have a dial-style thermostat, check to see if it contains mercury by carefully removing the front plastic round cover. If you see a small, sealed glass vial of silver liquid, that's mercury. Consider calling a professional to change your thermostat to an electronic model. When old-fashioned thermostats break in the home, they release very tiny droplets of mercury that evaporate and expose the occupants to the substance. In cases where thermometers and barometers break in a school or laboratory, the area needs to be evacuated and cleaned up by a professional. Mercury vapor can only be measured with the use of highly sensitive air-monitoring devices. Observe the following EPA cleanup guidelines for liquid mercury.

What Never to Do after a Mercury Spill

- Never use a vacuum cleaner to clean up mercury. The vacuum will put mercury into the air and increase exposure.
- Never use a broom to clean up mercury. It will break the mercury into smaller droplets and spread them.
- Never pour mercury down a drain. It may lodge in the plumbing and cause problems during future plumbing repairs. If discharged, it can pollute the septic tank or sewage-treatment plant.

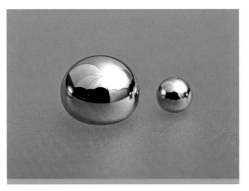

Liquid mercury may be found in thermometers and thermostats.

- Never wash clothing or other items that have come into direct contact with mercury in a washing machine, because mercury may contaminate the machine or pollute sewage. Clothing that has come into direct contact with mercury—that is, mercury has been spilled directly on the clothing—should be discarded.
- Never walk around your house while wearing shoes that might be contaminated with mercury. Contaminated clothing can also spread mercury.

What to Do If a Mercury Thermometer Breaks

NOTE: These instructions also apply to spills from other sources, if the amount spilled is less than or similar to the amount in a thermometer.

- Have everyone else leave the area; don't let anyone walk through the mercury on their way out. Remove all pets from the area. Open all windows and doors to the outside and shut all doors to other parts of the house.
- *Do not* allow children to help you clean up the spill.
- Attempt to remove mercury from the following surfaces: sealed or painted wood, linoleum, tile, and any similarly smooth surfaces. Po-

rous surfaces such as carpeting or fabric make recovery very difficult. In these instances, the area will need to be removed (cut out) and properly disposed of.

- Throw away any contaminated carpet, curtains, upholstery, or other absorbent surfaces in accordance with the disposal means outlined below. Cut out and remove the affected portion of the contaminated carpet for disposal.

Items Needed to Perform Small Mercury Cleanup Activities

- 4–5 Ziplock-type bags
- trash bags (2 to 6 mm thick)
- rubber, nitrile, or latex gloves
- paper towels
- cardboard or squeegee
- eyedropper
- duct tape, or shaving cream and small paintbrush
- flashlight
- powdered sulfur (optional)

Cleanup Instructions

1. Put on rubber, nitrile, or latex gloves.
2. Carefully pick up any broken pieces of glass or sharp objects. Place all broken objects on a damp paper towel. Fold the paper towel and place it in a Ziplock-type bag. Secure the bag and label it as di-

rected by your local health or fire department.

3. Locate visible mercury beads and use a squeegee or piece of cardboard to gather them. Make slow sweeping motions to keep mercury from becoming uncontrollable. Hold a flashlight at a low angle close to the floor in a darkened room to look for additional glistening beads of mercury that may be sticking to the surface or in small cracked areas of the surface. *Note:* Mercury can move surprising distances on hard and flat surfaces, so inspect the entire room carefully.

4. Collect or draw up the mercury beads with an eyedropper. Slowly and carefully squeeze the beads onto a damp paper towel. Place the paper towel in a Ziplock-type bag and secure it. Label the bag as directed by your local health or fire department.

5. Dab shaving cream on top of a small paintbrush and gently "dot" the affected area to pick up smaller, hard-to-see beads. Alternatively, use duct tape to collect smaller hard-to-see beads. Place the paintbrush or duct tape in a Ziplock-type bag bag and secure it. Label the bag as directed by your local health or fire department.

6. OPTIONAL STEP: Use commercially available powdered sulfur to absorb the beads that are too small to see. The sulfur makes the mercury easier to see, because it may change the color from yellow to brown, it binds the mercury for easier removal, and it suppresses the vapor of any missing mercury. Commercial sulfur may be supplied as mercury-vapor absorbent in mercury-spill kits, which can be purchased from laboratory, chemical-supply, and hazardous materials–response supply manufacturers. *Note:* Powdered sulfur may stain fabrics a dark color. When using powdered sulfur, do not breathe in the powder, as it can be moderately toxic. Additionally, carefully read and understand product information before use.

7. Consider requesting the services of a contractor who has monitoring equipment to screen for mercury vapors. Consult your local environmental or health agency to inquire about contractors in your area. Place all materials used during the cleanup, including gloves, in a trash bag along with the mercury beads and contaminated objects. Secure the trash bag and label it as directed by your local health or fire department.

8. Contact your local health department, municipal-waste authority, or fire department for proper disposal in accordance with local, state, and federal laws.
9. Keep the area well ventilated to the outside (that is, keep windows open and fans in exterior windows running) for at least twenty-four hours after your successful cleanup. Continue to keep pets and children out of the cleanup area. If sickness occurs, seek medical attention immediately.

Danger: Compact Fluorescent Lights

Compact fluorescent lights (CFLs) are becoming much more common in homes today, as they last longer and are much more energy efficient than traditional incandescent bulbs. Each lightbulb contains a small amount of mercury dust that aids in illumination. If the bulb breaks, the mercury dust is released. Don't dismiss this exposure. Adhere to the following EPA guidelines for responding to a broken CFL:

- Have people and pets leave the room, and don't let anyone walk through the breakage area on their way out.
- Open a window and leave the room for fifteen minutes or more.
- Shut off the central-air heating or air-conditioning system, if you have one.

Cleanup Steps for Hard Surfaces

- Do not use a vacuum or broom to clean up the broken bulb on hard surfaces. Common household vacuums and dry sweeping activities will allow mercury dust to become

A common compact fluorescent lightbulb

airborne, creating an inhalation hazard.

- Carefully scoop up glass pieces and powder using stiff paper or cardboard and place them in a glass jar with a metal lid (such as a canning jar) or in a sealed plastic bag.
- Pick up any remaining small glass fragments and powder with tape.
- Wipe the area clean with damp paper towels or disposable wet wipes. Place the towels in the glass jar or plastic bag.

Cleanup Steps for Carpeting or Rugs

- Carefully pick up glass fragments and place them in a glass jar with a metal lid (such as a canning jar) or in a sealed plastic bag.
- Pick up any remaining small glass fragments and powder with tape.
- If vacuuming is needed after all visible materials are removed, vacuum the area where the bulb was broken.
- Remove the vacuum bag (or empty and wipe the canister) and put the bag or vacuum debris in a sealed plastic bag.

Cleanup Steps for Clothing, Bedding, and Other Soft Materials

- Throw away any clothing or bedding materials that have come into direct contact with broken glass or mercury-containing powder from inside the bulb that may stick to the fabric. Do not wash such clothing or bedding, because mercury fragments in the clothing may contaminate the machine or pollute sewage.
- Wash clothing or other materials that have been exposed to the mercury vapor from a broken CFL, such as the clothing you are wearing when you cleaned up the broken CFL, as long as that clothing has not come into direct contact with the materials from the broken bulb.
- If your shoes come into direct contact with broken glass or mercury-containing powder from the bulb, wipe them off with damp paper towels or disposable wet wipes. Place the towels or wipes in a glass jar or sealed plastic bag for disposal.

Disposal of Cleanup Materials

- Check with your local or state government agencies about disposal requirements in your specific area. Some states do not allow such trash disposal, but instead require that broken and unbroken mercury-containing bulbs be taken to a local recycling center.

Future Cleaning of Carpeting or Rug: Air Out the Room During and after Vacuuming

- The next several times you vacuum, shut off the central-air heating or air-conditioning system and open a window before vacuuming.

- Keep the central-air heating or air-conditioning system shut off and the window open for at least fifteen minutes after vacuuming is completed.

Danger: Mold

Mold, which is a fungus, comes in all shapes, sizes, and colors and is found in the natural environment. Some molds are more likely to cause health problems than others. The mold growing in your shower, around your window, or in your furnace is not desirable. Associated health effects can include asthma, allergic reactions, or even serious fungal respiratory infections. Those who are at greatest risk include infants and children, elderly people, individuals with respiratory conditions or allergies, and people with weakened immune systems.

Mold needs moisture to grow, so controlling moisture is where prevention starts. Bathrooms, window sills, and the insides of dehumidifiers are all areas where mold can grow. The best way to determine whether you have a mold problem is to use your eyes and nose. Visible discoloration and a musty, rank odor are indications you may have a mold problem. Testing for mold tells you little about the connection between mold presence and possible health problems.

To clean up and remove indoor mold growth, the Minnesota Department of Health recommends that you follow steps 1 through 8, presented below, as they apply to your home:

Mold in a bathroom shower. Yuck!

1. **Identify and fix the moisture problem** The most important step in solving a mold problem is to identify and correct the moisture source(s) that allowed the growth in the first place. Common indoor moisture sources include:
- flooding
- condensation (caused by indoor humidity that is too high or surfaces that are too cold)
- roof and plumbing leaks
- firewood stored indoors
- humidifier use
- inadequate ventilation of kitchen and bath humidity
- improper ventilation of combustion appliances
- failure to vent clothes dryer exhaust outdoors (including electric dryers)
- clothesline drying indoors

   To keep indoor surfaces as dry as possible, try to maintain the home's relative humidity between 20 and 40 percent in the winter and lower than 60 percent the rest of the year. You can purchase devices to measure relative humidity at some home-supply stores. Ventilation, air circulation near cold surfaces, dehumidification, and efforts to minimize the production of moisture in the home are all very important in controlling high humidity, which frequently causes mold growth in cold climates.

2. **Begin drying all wet materials** As soon as possible after areas become wet, use fans and dehumidifiers and move wet items away from walls and off floors. Check with equipment-rental companies or restoration firms for additional equipment or contracting options.

3. **Remove and dispose of mold-contaminated materials** Items that have absorbed moisture and that have mold growing on them need to be removed, bagged, and thrown out. Such materials may include sheet rock, insulation, plaster, carpet/carpet pad, ceiling tiles, wood products (other than solid wood), and paper products. Likewise, any such porous materials that have come into contact with sewage should also be bagged and thrown away. Nonporous materials with surface mold growth may be saved if they are cleaned well and kept dry (see step 4).

4. **Take steps to protect yourself** The number of mold particles in the air can increase greatly when mold is disturbed. Consider wearing personal protective equipment (PPE) when handling or working

around mold-contaminated materials. The following equipment can help minimize exposure to mold:

- rubber gloves
- eye goggles
- outer clothing (long sleeves and long pants) that can be easily removed in the work area and laundered or discarded
- an N95- or a N100-type disposable respirator, specifically designed to protect the user from dust and particulates. Where mold growth is very heavy or covers an extensive area, or if you are sensitive to airborne contaminants, greater respiratory protection may be more appropriate. More protective options include half-face negative-air respirators with HEPA filters (N100 or P100).

5. **Take steps to protect others**
   Plan and perform all work to minimize the amount of dust generated. Where possible, consider the following actions to help minimize the spread of mold spores:

- Enclose or contain all moldy materials in plastic bags or sheets before carrying them through your home.
- Hang plastic sheeting to separate the work area from the rest of your home.

- Cover supply and return vents in the work area.
- Place fans in windows of the work area to pull contaminated air out of the work area and exhaust it to the outdoors.
- Remove your outer layer of work clothing in the work area and wash it separately or bag it for disposal.
- Damp clean the entire work area to pick up settled mold spores and dust.

6. **Clean surfaces** Surface mold growing on nonporous or semi-porous materials, such as hard plastic, concrete, glass, metal, and solid wood, can usually be cleaned. Cleaning to remove and capture all mold contamination is very important, because dead spores and mold particles may cause health problems if they are left in place.

- Thoroughly scrub all contaminated surfaces using a stiff brush, hot water, and a nonammonia soap or commercial cleaner.
- Collect any excess cleaning liquid with a wet-dry vacuum, mop, or sponge.
- Rinse the area with clean water and collect the excess rinse water.

7. **Disinfect surfaces (if desired)**
   After removing all visible mold and other soil from contaminated surfaces, apply a disinfectant to

kill mold missed by the cleaning. In the case of sewage contamination, disinfection is strongly suggested—contact your local health department for appropriate advice.

- Mix one-quarter to one-half cup of bleach per gallon of water, and apply the solution to surfaces where mold growth was visible before cleaning. Apply the solution with a sponge or by other methods that do not oversaturate or flood the surface area.

- Collect any excess bleach solution with a clean and filtered wet-dry vacuum, sponge, or mop. Do not rinse or wipe the bleach solution off the areas being treated—allow it to dry on the surface.

  Always handle bleach with caution. *Never mix bleach with ammonia—toxic chlorine gas may result.* Bleach can irritate the eyes, nose, throat, and skin. Introduce fresh air into the work area (for example, open a window or door). Protect your skin and eyes from contact with bleach. Test the solution on a small area before treatment, because bleach is very corrosive and may damage some materials.

8. **Remain on mold alert** Continue looking for signs of moisture problems or the return of mold growth. Be particularly alert to moisture in areas of past growth. If mold returns, repeat the previous cleaning steps and consider using a stronger solution to disinfect the area again. Regrowth may signal that the material should be removed or that moisture is not yet controlled.

Danger: Radon

The Minnesota State Health Department provides the following information about radon gas.

What Is Radon?

Radon is a naturally occurring radioactive gas that continuously decays and releases radiation. It is produced from minerals in soil, such as uranium and radium, and it is colorless, odorless, and tasteless. The presence of and threat to your home from radon gas is therefore dependent on your local geology. To determine whether your home may be at risk, check with your local health department and county or state geological agency or society.

Why Is Radon Important?

The EPA estimates that each year, twenty-one thousand people die of lung cancer as a result of being exposed to elevated levels of radon. Radon is the second-leading cause of lung cancer for smokers and the leading cause of lung cancer for non-smokers.

Although radon is present throughout the environment, radon levels indoors are generally higher and therefore increase the risk of cancer.

How Does Radon Enter a Home?

Radon is a gas that moves though spaces in the soil or fill material around a home's foundation. Certain homes tend to operate under a negative pressure, especially in the lowest portions of the home and during the times of year when the furnace is operating. A negative pressure situation occurs when the windows and doors in the home are closed and the operation of the furnace creates a vacuum—sucking in the air around it. This negative vacuum pulls soil gases, including radon, into the lower level of the structure. Some causes of home vacuum include the following:

- heated air rising inside the home (stack effect)
- wind blowing past a home (down-wind draft effect)
- air used by fireplaces, wood stoves, and furnaces (vacuum effect)
- air vented to the outside by clothes dryers and exhaust fans in bathrooms, kitchens, or attics (vacuum effect)

Radon can enter a home through the floor and walls—anywhere there is an opening between the home and the soil (see Figure 12.1). Examples of such openings include dirt-floor crawl spaces, unsealed sumps, cracks in slab-on-grade floors, utility penetrations, and tiny pores in concrete block walls. A basement, of course, provides a large surface area that is in direct contact with soil material.

What Happens after Radon Gets into the Home?

Once radon enters a home, it moves freely throughout the air, and people breathe it into their lungs, where it can cause cell damage that may lead to lung cancer. Understanding how it moves through the home environment can help explain why timing and location are important factors to consider when conducting a radon test.

The level of radon is often highest in the lowest part of the building.

FIGURE 12.1 Major Radon Entry Routes

A. cracks in concrete slabs

B. spaces behind brick veneer walls that rest on uncapped hollow-block foundations

C. pores and cracks in concrete blocks

D. floor-wall joints

E. exposed soil, as in a sump or crawl space

F. weeping (drain) tile, if drained to an open sump

G. mortar joints

H. loose-fitting pipe penetrations

I. open tops of block walls

J. building materials, such as brick, concrete, or rock

K. well water (not commonly a major source in Minnesota homes)

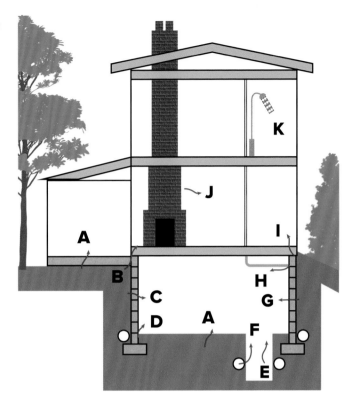

Radon moves through a house via diffusion and natural air movements, and it can be distributed by mechanical equipment, such as a forced-air ventilation system. As radon moves away from the home's foundation or other entry points, it mixes with and is diluted into a greater volume of air. In addition, more dilution occurs in the upper levels of the home that offer more fresh-air ventilation.

Greater dilution and less of a vacuum may also occur when the house is more open to the outdoors during the nonheating season. In other words, indoor radon levels are typically lower in the summer than compared to the winter.

How Can You Find Out Whether or Not Your Home Has a Radon Problem?

A radon test is the only way to find out how much radon is in your home. Performing a radon test on your own is easy, inexpensive, and can be done privately. Every home is unique due to its local soil, construction details, maintenance, and degree of pressurization. Therefore, test results from nearby homes cannot be relied upon to predict the radon level in another home. Likewise, previous test results may not reflect the current and future radon levels for a home that has been remodeled or weatherized or has had changes to its heating, air-conditioning, or other ventilation systems, such as the installation of exhaust fans.

State health departments often recommend that homeowners test their homes for radon. The results of a properly performed radon test will help you determine for yourself whether or not you need to take further action to protect your family from the health risks of radon. Contact your local health department agency for recommendations for radon testing kits.

Danger: Asbestos

The Minnesota State Health Department offers the following information regarding asbestos in the home.

What Is Asbestos?

Asbestos is a naturally occurring mineral fiber mined from the earth. It is heat and chemical resistant and easily formed into just about any shape or

Asbestos mineral fiber occurs naturally and is still mined for many industrial applications.

product. Prior to the 1970s it was commonly used in more than three thousand different construction materials and manufactured products, including many found in homes, such as floor tile, ceiling tile, and insulation.

Why Is It a Concern?

When disturbed, asbestos breaks down into very small fibers up to 1,200 times thinner than a human hair. These tiny fibers easily become airborne, and, when inhaled, they can travel deep into the lungs and become trapped in lung tissue. Once trapped, these fibers can cause mesothelioma, lung cancer, and asbestosis. There's no known safe level of asbestos exposure, and medical research indicates these fibers can cause severe lung diseases and cancer ten to thirty years after the initial asbestos exposure. Therefore, it is important to identify asbestos-containing materials in your home so you can protect your health as well as the health of your family.

What Products Contain Asbestos?

The following is a short list of some of the more common asbestos-containing materials found in homes:

- adhesives
- appliance components
- ceiling products
  - ceiling texture (popcorn texture)
  - ceiling tiles
  - ceiling tile mastic
- cement-asbestos board (Transite) products
  - chimney-flue lining
  - ducts
  - pipes
  - shingles
  - siding
  - wall panels
- electrical products
  - cloth-wire insulation
  - electrical panels
- flooring products
  - asphalt floor tiles
  - floor-tile mastic
  - vinyl floor tiles
  - vinyl-sheet flooring (linoleum)
- heating and cooling system products
  - boiler insulation
  - duct-work insulation
  - furnace insulation
  - gaskets
  - heat shields (paper and corrugated cardboard)
  - pipe insulation
  - tank insulation
- paints and coatings
- plaster
- roofing products
  - base flashing
  - felt
  - shingles
  - tar, or "Black Jack"
- table pads
- vermiculite
  - attic and wall insulation
  - fireplace decoration
  - gardening products
- vinyl wall coverings
- wall applications
  - caulking and putties
  - spackling compounds
- wallboard or sheetrock
- wallboard joint compound
- window glazing

How Do You Find Out Whether or Not It Is Asbestos?

You can check for asbestos markings on the material or its packaging or hire a certified asbestos inspector to sample the material or perform an asbestos inspection. Certified contractors can be found through the EPA (see the URL for this website at the end of this chapter under "Resources").

Aren't All Asbestos Products Banned?

The EPA has only banned the use of the following asbestos-containing products:

- spray-applied material
- pipe insulation
- boilers and water-heater insulation
- various paper and sheet products

What to Do If You Have Asbestos in Your Home

Leave it alone!—Asbestos is only a problem if asbestos fibers are released into the air. If the asbestos material is in good condition and is not being disturbed, it will not release asbestos fibers. The safest and least costly option may be to leave the asbestos material alone.

Repair it—Sometimes asbestos materials can be repaired. If the asbestos material has minimal damage, it may be repaired with a special coating called encapsulant. Check with your hardware store or a safety-supply store for materials to repair or seal asbestos.

Remove it—Removing the asbestos material may be the best option if it is extensively damaged or will be disturbed by renovation or other activities. Homeowners may legally remove asbestos materials themselves from single-family homes they own and occupy. However, health departments strongly recommend using a licensed or certified asbestos contractor. Licensed or certified contractors use techniques that are unfamiliar to homeowners, ensuring the asbestos is handled safely. They also perform air-monitoring tests to determine whether the air in your home meets acceptable standards during and after the project.

RESOURCES

EPA information regarding lead-paint exposure and renovation in the home can be found at http://www.epa.gov/lead/pubs/renovation.htm.

The EPA has a website to help people find a certified lead repair, renovation, or painting contractor in your state at http://www.epa.gov/lead/pubs/lscp-renovation_firm.htm.

 EPA mercury cleanup recommendations can be found at http://www.epa.gov/hg/spills.

 The EPA list of health effects due to mercury exposure can be found at http://www.epa.gov/mercury/effects.htm#elem.

The EPA website regarding asbestos-containing material can be found at http://www.epa.gov/asbestos.

The Minnesota Health Department, Environmental Health Division can be found at http://www.health.state.mn.us/divs/eh.

 For assistance in selecting indoor air-quality professionals, review the following:

- American Council for Accredited Certification (under "Find Certificants"): http://www.acac.org/find/database.aspx.
- Indoor Air Quality Association: http://www.iaqa.org/member_listings/members_new.asp.
- American Industrial Hygiene Association: https://webportal.aiha.org/Custom/ConsultantsSearch.aspx.
- American Board of Industrial Hygiene: http://www.abih.org/members/roster/rostersearch.cfm.
- Institute of Inspection Cleaning and Restoration Certification: http://www.certifiedcleaners.org/locator.shtml.

I post current home-safety articles and information on my website at http://www.danshomesafety.com.

CHAPTER 13

Working and Playing in the Yard

KCK homeowner killed in trench collapse—man trying to repair sewer line gets trapped in ditch

A 39-year-old homeowner was killed Friday afternoon while working in an 8-foot ditch in his yard. Fire Chief Craig Duke said Joseph Laster and a plumber were trying to repair a sewer line in the back yard at 1728 Haskell Ave. when the trench collapsed, trapping Laster.

— KMBC.com, Kansas City, KS, 23 January 2009

Few activities are more satisfying than returning to yard work in the spring. A winter's worth of planning and the first hints of warm weather beg you to go outside for fresh air, some work, and some play. However, your backyard environment presents safety and health hazards that you are not exposed to inside.

Working in the Yard

Yard work brings into play many of the safety practices already covered in this book. Working outside exposes you to chemical hazards, power-tool

hazards, lifting injuries, falls, electrical hazards, and the need to use personal protective equipment properly. However, as explained in this chapter, additional hazards await you as you step outside. Enjoy your home's surroundings, but keep your safety knowledge close at hand!

Buried Utilities

Before you plant a tree, dig a hole for deck footing, or drive a post for a birdhouse, you need to know what's underground. Water lines, sewer lines, electrical cables, and gas utilities are often buried. Buried utilities have been struck at depths as shallow as one foot below the ground. A shovel, post-hole digger, or pick axe can do as much damage as an excavation machine. It only takes one swing with a hand tool to hit a natural gas line and cause an explosion.

Nearly every state has a "call-before-you-dig" law. The person digging (contractor or homeowner) must call a hotline to help locate utilities. The national number to call before you dig is 811. Your local utility provider will send a technician to mark the approximate location of the utility. Despite this requirement, contractors still strike thousands of utilities each year in the United States, causing deaths and millions of dollars of

The law requires you to check for the location of utilities, by dialing 811, before you dig.

damage. This occurs when contractors fail to request utility locations by dialing 811, they work too hastily, or the utilities are not accurately marked. Paint markings or small colored flags approximate the location of the utility within about two feet on either side of the line.

The locate service is free and can take up to forty-eight hours. Plan ahead! Don't dig until all utilities have been located. Note that the utility locate service may not locate utilities on your property. For instance, the underground natural gas service line that runs from the street to your home

(Image courtesy of the Common Ground Alliance)

may be marked by a yellow painted line or flag (see Figure 13.1 below for the colors used to mark different utilities). The markings may stop on your property, particularly if the direction of the utility cannot be followed. In this case, do *not* assume that the utility continues on a straight path. Additionally, the previous owner may have relocated or moved the service utility line. Do not guess the locations of your utilities.

Uniform Color Code

WHITE: Proposed excavation

PINK: Temporary survey markings

RED: Electric power lines, cables, conduit and lighting cables

YELLOW: Gas, oil, steam, petroleum or gaseous materials

ORANGE: Communication, alarm or signal lines, cables or conduit

BLUE: Potable water

PURPLE: Reclaimed water, irrigation and slurry lines

GREEN: Sewers and drain lines

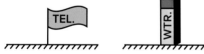

FIGURE 13.1 The conventional colors for marking utilities

Excavation Safety

Once you've located utilities, you can break ground. Dig carefully. Home-

owners are severely injured or killed each year in backyard hand-dug trenches that collapse on them. Each cubic yard of soil (three feet by three feet by three feet) weighs between two thousand and three thousand pounds. Digging yourself out when buried up to your knees is difficult, and when buried up to your waist, it is impossible. Because soil is made up of varying amounts of sand, silt, clay, organic matter, and water moisture, its ability to hold together can vary from one part of your yard to another. A hole or trench has a natural tendency to slump, or to "self-level." To counteract this tendency, a hole or trench needs to be dug at an appropriate angle.

Never climb into a trench or hole that has not been angled or sloped at a 1-to-1.5 ratio or greater. For every foot of depth you dig down, you must also dig back from the bottom of the hole or trench 1.5 feet.

Example: For a trench dug 5 feet deep and 4 feet wide at the base, the amount of space across the top would need to be 19 feet, or 7.5 (1.5×5 on left side) + 4 (bottom) + 7.5 (1.5×5 on right side) = 19. See Figure 13.2 for a diagram. Plan ahead for space!

The following excavation practices are recommended:

- Never work alone in a trench, especially one deeper than three

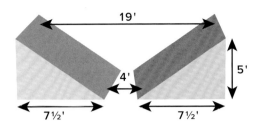

FIGURE 13.2 An example of a safe trench

feet. Always have someone outside the trench available to summon help.

- Consider hiring a professional contractor to complete your excavation work.

- Watch out for conditions that make the soil less stable and susceptible to collapse:
  - rain or ground water
  - vibrating equipment (power tools, idling heaving equipment, and so forth)
  - soil piled next to the hole, which creates additional pressure on the sidewall, pushing it inward and downward
- Consider renting protective-shield equipment (called a trench box) if you don't have enough room to properly slope the excavation.

Photo courtesy of My Construction Photos

Overhead Electrical Lines

You have to be aware of not only what is beneath but also what is overhead. Contact with overhead power lines injures and kills hundreds of homeowners every year. This hazard is also addressed in Chapter 5, "Electrical Hazards." Observe the following precautions when working near overhead power lines:

- Stay at least ten feet from the line.

Don't forget to look up to spot overhead power lines.

Electrical service entering the home right above the back door can present a hazard if working with an extension ladder or a long-handled tool.

This includes your body and any tools or equipment you may be using, such as an extension ladder. The black coating you see on the line is often worn and is *not* an insulator, so it will *not* protect you from shock.

- Never approach a downed power line. Contact the utility company to alert a professional about downed lines.
- If you have to work closer than ten feet from your power line, contact the electrical utility company to help you shield your work from the line or to schedule a time to turn off the power to the line.
- Don't guess whether the line overhead is an electrical line or a telephone line. Call the electrical utility company to find out for sure. Just because you see birds sitting on the wires does not mean it is safe!

Dealing With Bites, Stings, Plants, and Burns

For most people, a bee sting or bite from a wood tick is harmless, but others can experience a life-threatening allergic reaction or contract a crippling joint disease, such as Lyme's disease. Bees, ticks, plants, spiders,

A common wood tick

This is a poison ivy leaf. Learn to identify poisonous plants.

snakes—all of these biological hazards are often overlooked but present significant health risks. Apply bug repellent as needed, be mindful of other people who are allergic to stings or bites, and stock your first-aid kit accordingly.

Such plants as poison oak, poison ivy, or poison sumac can turn a fun day in the yard or woods into a miserable event that may even necessitate a trip to the doctor. Oils from these plants are difficult to remove from the skin and clothing. Wear appropriate clothing to protect yourself and remember that clothing will absorb the oil. If you know you've been working around these plants, do not place contaminated clothes in the washing machine, as this will transfer the oil to other clothes. Consider discarding the clothing, and if you need to complete further work in the same area, wear a disposable coverall suit such as one made of Tyvec. Do *not* burn poisonous plants, because the oil will aerosolize and drift with the smoke. Inhaling smoke can result in a severe respiratory emergency. Learn how to identify the most common poisonous plants and take action accordingly.

Protect Against Sun and Heat

Finally, don't forget about the sun. Your chances of contracting skin cancer increase each time you receive a moderate to severe sunburn. Cover your body, including your head, or apply sunscreen with a sun protection factor (SPF) rating greater than 30. Re-apply it every several hours or more frequently if you sweat.

When the temperature and humidity are both high, take frequent breaks in the shade and drink plenty of water and drinks containing electrolytes. If you stop sweating, that is a sign of dehydration and possibly heat exhaustion. Without treatment, symptoms get worse and lead to the possibility of heatstroke—a critical medical emergency. Pace yourself in the heat and start work in the early morning. Plan your work around available shade as the sun moves through the day.

Playing in the Yard

To get an idea of the dangers associated with a playset, trampoline, and swimming pool, all you have to do is watch an episode of *America's Funniest Home Videos*. There you'll see children and teenagers (and sometimes adults) intentionally pushing their abilities to the limit by performing stunts. These outdoor pieces of equipment beg young people to behave recklessly. Supervision is a must, but you can't be everywhere all the time. Kids are kids, and they will get hurt regardless of how diligent you are. Control what you can by making the safest backyard entertainment possible available to your kids (and the neighbors' kids, of course). If you choose to skip discussion on these three toys, please read the end of the chapter regarding head injuries.

Playsets

Playsets come in all shapes and sizes and provide a number of options for swinging, climbing, and sliding. Sets are most commonly made of wood and include metal and plastic hardware components. Consider the following safe practices around playsets:

- Take the time and care to assemble a playset according to the manufacturer's directions. Placing it on level ground and making sure it is stable and secured to the ground are key elements. If the playset gets heavy use, check it monthly to make sure all the bolts, screws, handles, and other hardware are tightly secured. Pay close attention to the wear spots, such as where a chain on a swing connects to an overhead support.

A typical backyard filled with play equipment

- Place a soft material, such as wood chips or sand, under all areas where a fall could occur, in order to soften the blow of a hard landing.

Trampoline

Your home-insurance premium goes up if you disclose to the insurance company that you own a trampoline, because trampolines can and do cause disabling injuries every year. A broken limb or even paralysis can occur if a person falls from a trampoline. Consider the following safe practices for trampolines:

- Maintain the trampoline according to the manufacturer's recommendations. In time, the fabric and springs wear out, especially if the trampoline is left outside in the elements year-round. Based on the manufacturer's recommendations, determine when it is time to replace the fabric or springs *before* excessive wear and failure occur.
- Place the trampoline on level, stable ground.
- Consider the purchase of an add-on cage enclosure that prevents the jumpers from bouncing off the trampoline. Only purchase and install a cage that has been approved by the manufacturer.

Swimming Pools

Swimming pools offer a relaxing, cool way to enjoy the hot weather. Unfortunately, every year children drown while being "supervised" by older siblings or adults who were distracted only for a minute. Consider the following pool-safety guidelines:

- Closely supervise swimmers who are inexperienced or cannot touch the bottom of any part of the pool. Do not lose sight of any of the swimmers and be sure to know how to swim and perform rescues yourself if needed.
- Never let anyone swim alone; always be sure someone is in attendance.
- Do not allow diving (head first) unless the pool is deep enough to allow for it. Head and neck injuries result in paralysis, so jump in feet first.
- Do not allow the use of any hard toys or toys that can result in someone getting entangled.
- Make sure personal flotation devices, such as life vests, are the proper size and are properly fitted for young swimmers, and make sure that the swimmers who need them use them.

Head Injuries

Trauma to the head is particularly troublesome, as it can leave no apparent sign of injury yet cause symptoms to appear days or weeks later. Everyone responds differently to an injury to the head that may be caused by sports, an automobile accident, or a home injury.

A personal story: On a Sunday in May 2011, while I was at a playground with my three-and-a-half-year-old daughter, she fell, hitting her head on a step of the playset. She cried immediately, never lost consciousness, and ran to me with a cut to the back of her head. The bleeding was significant, so a trip to the ER ensued. Three staples later she was sent home with instructions for me to wake her at 2:00 AM and to watch for any abnormal behavior. Three days later while she was at day care, she stumbled over the edge of a sandbox and fell on her hip. The fall was fairly normal, but day-care staff reported that she lapsed into a mild seizure. Her eyes rolled back, her breathing was a bit erratic, and she shook slightly. My wife and I were called and immediately took her to the hospital. A CT scan showed no obvious hemorrhage or tumor, so we were advised to seek an evaluation for epileptic seizures. On Wednesday of that week, my daughter spent nearly five hours completing an EEG exam at a specialty clinic. Twenty-four electrodes were attached to her head to measure brain-wave patterns while testing her reactions to light stimulus and during sleep. The test showed no lingering effects of the mild seizure.

We were told that the head injury she sustained and the associated seizure could be insignificant or the beginning of a life-long condition of being prone to further seizures, which is frightening, because each time a person lapses into a seizure, brain cells die.

I'm not asking you to coddle your child and not let them play rough and enjoy life. Again, control what you can and take reasonable steps to be safe. With high-risk activities (biking, skateboarding, roller blading, ice skating, and so forth), make sure children wear helmets. Like all safety equipment, helmets need to be properly sized, fitted, and worn during every activity.

My trooper Laura at the end of her **EEG** exam, tired and frustrated

Child Safety

Children's lack of life experience, their curiosity, and their need to have fun make them considerably more vulnerable to accidents. Most children make poor choices when it comes to safety. It is tough enough to get a young person to try a new vegetable at the dinner table, let alone getting them to be safe. For this reason, take extra care when it comes to safeguarding your house for your children. As much as you believe that you can think like a child and anticipate what they might get into, you will almost always be fooled. How can you prevent kids from jumping on the bed or couch? You can't! Children will fall out of trees, be impaled by their own toys, swallow their toys, and do just about any other risky behavior until they've learned their lesson—sound familiar?

The hazards presented throughout this book are equal-opportunity sources of injury—age does not matter. The "big four" hazards that present the greatest danger to children include electricity, falls, burns, and poisoning. Educating a youngster about the importance of safety is a lifelong commitment. In the meantime, the key principles of child safety include preventing access to and coming into direct contact with a hazard. This is a simple concept, but it only takes one momentary lapse in vigilance to result in an injury or even death. Every year, news stations feature reports of people leaving infants in bathtubs "only for a minute," resulting in drowning.

You can't be everywhere all the time to safeguard your children, but you must be reasonably diligent. They will get hurt, and they will try to get into places they know they shouldn't. Safety solutions must be in place at all times to be successful. Consider the following basics for preventing access to and contact with these hazards:

- Electrical
  - Unplug appliances not in use.
  - Keep in-use electrical cords out of reach of infants, especially those who like to bite. You may think that cords are hidden, but your children will find them. Rather, barricade them by placing heavy items over the tops of cords or running cords behind large objects that cannot be moved or accessed.
  - If cords absolutely cannot be moved or barricaded, make sure outlets are protected with a GFCI device to prevent against accidental shock.
  - Plug all unused outlets with plastic caps to prevent little fingers from being inserted.
- Burns
  - Limit access to sources of open flame or hot objects (irons, stove burners, fireplaces, and so forth) by placing swing gates across doorways leading into hazardous areas, such as the kitchen. Install guard or shield devices in front of fireplaces and on the stove to prevent children from reaching pots, burners, or control knobs.
  - Close and lock doors leading into areas that may include hot objects, such as the furnace or laundry room.
  - Keep all sources of fire (matches, lighters, and so forth) away from children, up high and in locked cabinets.
  - Hot water can be a source of thermal burns. Keep your hot water heater set at 120 degrees or cooler.

- Poisoning
  - Store chemicals and medicine in childproof containers, in high places, and behind locked doors. Ingesting chemicals or medications can result in the death of a child. Check your plants, as some may prove to be toxic when ingested, and keep the Poison Control number near the phone: (800) 222-1222.

- Falls
  - Use gates or other barriers to prevent infants from falling down the stairs.
  - Keep windows and doors locked to prevent unattended children from falling out of a window or off a balcony or deck.
  - Pick up toys and remove or cover furniture with sharp edges that may make an injury worse if a fall occurs.

RESOURCES

The Underground Safety Alliance assists communities and individuals in finding the locations of buried utilities. For more information go to http://usa811.org.

Safe Kids USA provides information for parents, teachers, and safety professionals that will help them improve toddler and child safety at http://www.safekids.org.

Children's Hospitals and Clinics of Minnesota provides information on a variety of child-safety topics at http://www.childrensmn.org/Services/Emergency/MakingSafeSimple.

I post current home-safety articles and information on my website at http://www.danshomesafety.com.

Appendix A: Hazard Hunt

Test your ability to spot and to correct a hazard. The "Hazard Hunt" activity is a favorite among construction workers, as they laugh at their industry comrades but also realize how lucky they've been, having done some of the same unsafe things. Some photos are from real project sites, while others are staged. Have fun!

For each of the photos, answer the following three questions:

1. What's unsafe? (there could be more than one item)
2. How could planning or performing a hazard analysis have prevented the unsafe situation?
3. How can the condition be corrected to make it safe?

The answers are at the end of the chapter.

1. A table saw

2. Building a new shed

4. Digging a trench to access a broken water connection to the house

3. Accessing the garage roof for maintenance

5. Replaced fuses in an electrical box

6. Fuel and oil containers in the basement

7. Additional electrical outlets needed outside

8. Mowing the grass

9. Cutting lumber with a circular saw

10. Protecting a power strip from water

11. Storage under the kitchen sink

Answers

Photo	What's Wrong?	Hazard Analysis or Planning Prevention	Make It Safe
1	No guard over the saw blade	Perform a safety check prior to use.	Install a guard over the blade according to manufacturer's requirements.
2	Stepping on top step of ladder	Determine working height and necessary ladder height.	Get a taller ladder.
3	Stepladder not being used in the open and locked position Ladder not on stable ground	Determine necessary working height and ladder height.	Use an extension ladder and place it on stable ground.
4	Hole not covered or guarded from pedestrian traffic No utility markings—did not locate utilities prior to start of project Excavation subject to cave-in because sidewalls are not sloped	Dial 811 to locate utilities at least two days prior to working. Working on or near a public utility requires permission. Determine dig depth and be prepared to slope the excavation or to have a contractor perform the work.	Stop! Request a utility locate. Barricade the hole when not in attendance and do not dig any deeper than waist height without proper sloping or cave-in protective systems.
5	Bolts being used instead of fuses (*extremely dangerous*)	Prior to the start of work, determine the size and type of fuse needed to complete the project.	Install a properly rated fuse.
6	Containers not labeled or marked Flammable and combustible liquids stored in the home	Inspect for labeling, spillage and container condition, and store in a proper location.	Label containers and place them in a fire-safe locker in the garage.
7	Third prong (ground) missing from plug Power strip not GFCI protected or rated for outdoor use	Check extension cords for damage or defects and rating of equipment prior to use.	Do not use equipment as shown. Purchase and use electrical equipment rated for outdoor use.

(cont'd.)

Answers (cont'd.)

Photo	What's Wrong?	Hazard Analysis or Planning Prevention	Make It Safe
8	No boots, safety glasses, or hearing protection Discharge chute tied up	Activity involves loud noise, flying debris, and rotating parts.	Wear PPE and use safety features (chute) properly as described by manufacturer.
9	Poor body positioning—bent at waist No hearing protection Power tool hazard—insufficient clearance for cutting with a circular saw	Determine proper work height and setup for power-tool use.	Utilize sawhorses to raise work height and achieve clearance for cut or work on stable blocks off the ground and kneel to get closer to the work. Use hearing protection.
10	Wrapping an electrical device in cellophane to keep it dry for outside use is not advisable	Determine electrical needs for outside project and purchase accordingly.	Replace this device immediately, as it provides poor grounding and GFCI protection.
11	Chemicals too easily accessible for children Water bottle in the front contains something other than water, isn't labeled, lacks childproof cap Fire extinguisher buried in the back and not easily accessible	Chemical storage should be high and locked if threat to children is present. Inspect secondary containers for labeling and check condition/location of fire extinguisher.	Move chemicals to a secure location. Label the water bottle to describe its true contents. Relocate the fire extinguisher.

Appendix B:
Master Inspection Schedule

The following table provides a recommended frequency for completing inspections throughout the home, inside and out. Feel free to copy this form and add categories as needed to make it your own. A check box present in a column indicates the recommended frequency for completing the inspection.

Year_____

System and Hazard Item (describe what and when)	How Often to Check	Condition		Date Hazard Corrected
		OK ✔	NOT OK ✘	
CHEMICAL				
Check chemical containers for readable labels and markings. Include secondary ("leftovers") containers.	Annually ☐ Jan 1			
Check that chemicals, including medications, are safely stored and secured from children. Make sure you are ready to handle a spill cleanup, including having the necessary PPE on hand.	Quarterly ☐ Jan 1 ☐ April 1 ☐ July 1 ☐ Oct 1			
ELECTRICAL				
Keep the circuit-breaker panel or fuse-box door closed and make sure the breakers are properly labeled and marked to identify circuits.	Annually ☐ Jan 1			

(cont'd.)

Master Inspection Schedule (cont'd.)

System and Hazard Item (describe what and when)	How Often to Check	Condition		Date Hazard Corrected
		OK ✔	NOT OK ✘	
Check outlets for scorched faceplates and test GFCI-protected outlets.	Semiannually ☐ Jan 1 ---- ☐ July 1			
Check extension cords for cuts, gouges, pinched areas, exposed wires, and so forth. Make sure the ground prong is in place on three-prong cords.	Quarterly ☐ Jan 1 ---- ☐ April 1 ---- ☐ July 1 ---- ☐ Oct 1			
Check power tools for general condition, including the cords.	Semiannually ☐ Jan 1 ---- ☐ July 1			
EMERGENCY PLANNING				
Check emergency provisions, such as bottled water, flashlights, and rations, to make sure they have not expired.	Semiannually ☐ Jan 1 ---- ☐ July 1			
FALLS				
If used, check personal fall-protection systems (anchorage point, rope, and so forth) to verify they are in good condition.	Before each use			
Check ladders for any damage, including the steps, braces, and locking mechanisms. Inspect for broken or nonworking items.	Before each use			

Master Inspection Schedule (cont'd.)

System and Hazard Item (describe what and when)	How Often to Check	Condition		Date Hazard Corrected
		OK ✔	NOT OK ✘	
Check stairway handrails, carpeting, treads, and risers for wear or damage and make sure they are firmly fixed in place.	Quarterly ☐ Jan 1 ☐ April 1 ☐ July 1 ☐ Oct 1			
Check outside thresholds, bathroom floors, and other areas where slips are likely to occur to make sure they are properly protected with non-slip coverings or coatings.	Quarterly ☐ Jan 1 ☐ April 1 ☐ July 1 ☐ Oct 1			
Check guardrail systems for loose or broken pieces.	Semiannually ☐ Jan 1 ☐ July 1			
Check items on shelving to make sure they are properly stacked and secured.	Quarterly ☐ Jan 1 ☐ April 1 ☐ July 1 ☐ Oct 1			
FIRE PREVENTION AND PREPAREDNESS				
Check ignition sources (flame, heat, static electricity) to make sure they are safely contained and associated appliances are working properly.	Semiannually ☐ Jan 1 ☐ July 1			
Store combustible materi-als safely away from ignition sources.	Semiannually ☐ Jan 1 ☐ July 1			

(cont'd.)

Master Inspection Schedule (cont'd.)

System and Hazard Item (describe what and when)	How Often to Check	Condition		Date Hazard Corrected
		OK ✔	NOT OK ✘	
Check fire extinguishers to make sure they are located where they are supposed to be, charged, accessible, and free of any damage.	Semiannually ☐ Jan 1 ☐ July 1			
Check smoke alarms to make sure they are working properly. Replace batteries (if equipped).	Semiannually ☐ Jan 1 ☐ July 1			
HAND AND POWER TOOLS				
Check for general condition and look for cracks, defects, worn power cords, missing screws, or anything else that may result in an unsafe condition.	Before each use			
INDOOR AIR QUALITY				
Check carbon-monoxide detectors for proper function according to the manufacturer's recommendations.	Quarterly ☐ Jan 1 ☐ April 1 ☐ July 1 ☐ Oct 1			
Check for signs of mold in common areas where warm, moist environments exist.	Quarterly ☐ Jan 1 ☐ April 1 ☐ July 1 ☐ Oct 1			

Master Inspection Schedule (cont'd.)

System and Hazard Item (describe what and when)	How Often to Check	Condition		Date Hazard Corrected
		OK ✔	NOT OK ✘	
PERSONAL PROTECTIVE EQUIPMENT				
Check safety glasses, gloves, boots, respirator, and all other items for wear and proper function.	Before each use			
UTILITIES INSIDE				
Check water valves, natural-gas valves, electrical circuits, and other utilities for labels and markings for easy identification.	Annually ☐ Jan 1			
UTILITIES OUTSIDE				
Each time prior to digging or working around overhead utilities, have them marked by the utility company—dial 811.	Before each use			
THE WEEKEND WARRIOR				
Check material-handling equipment (carts, dolly, wheelbarrow, and so forth) prior to use for signs of damage or wear.	Before each use			
WORKING AND PLAYING IN THE YARD				
Identify location of buried and overhead power utilities.	Before each use			

(cont'd.)

Master Inspection Schedule (cont'd.)

System and Hazard Item (describe what and when)	How Often to Check	Condition		Date Hazard Corrected
		OK ✔	NOT OK ✘	
Check condition of all play items, including playsets, trampolines, and swimming pools, according to the manufacturers' recommendations.	Annually ☐ Jan 1			